UNDERSTANDING & PREVENTING
SELF-HARM IN SCHOOLS

TINA RAE & JODY WALSHE

UNDERSTANDING & PREVENTING SELF-HARM IN SCHOOLS

Effective Strategies for Identifying Risk & Providing Support

HINTON HOUSE Therapeutic Resources

HINTONHOUSE

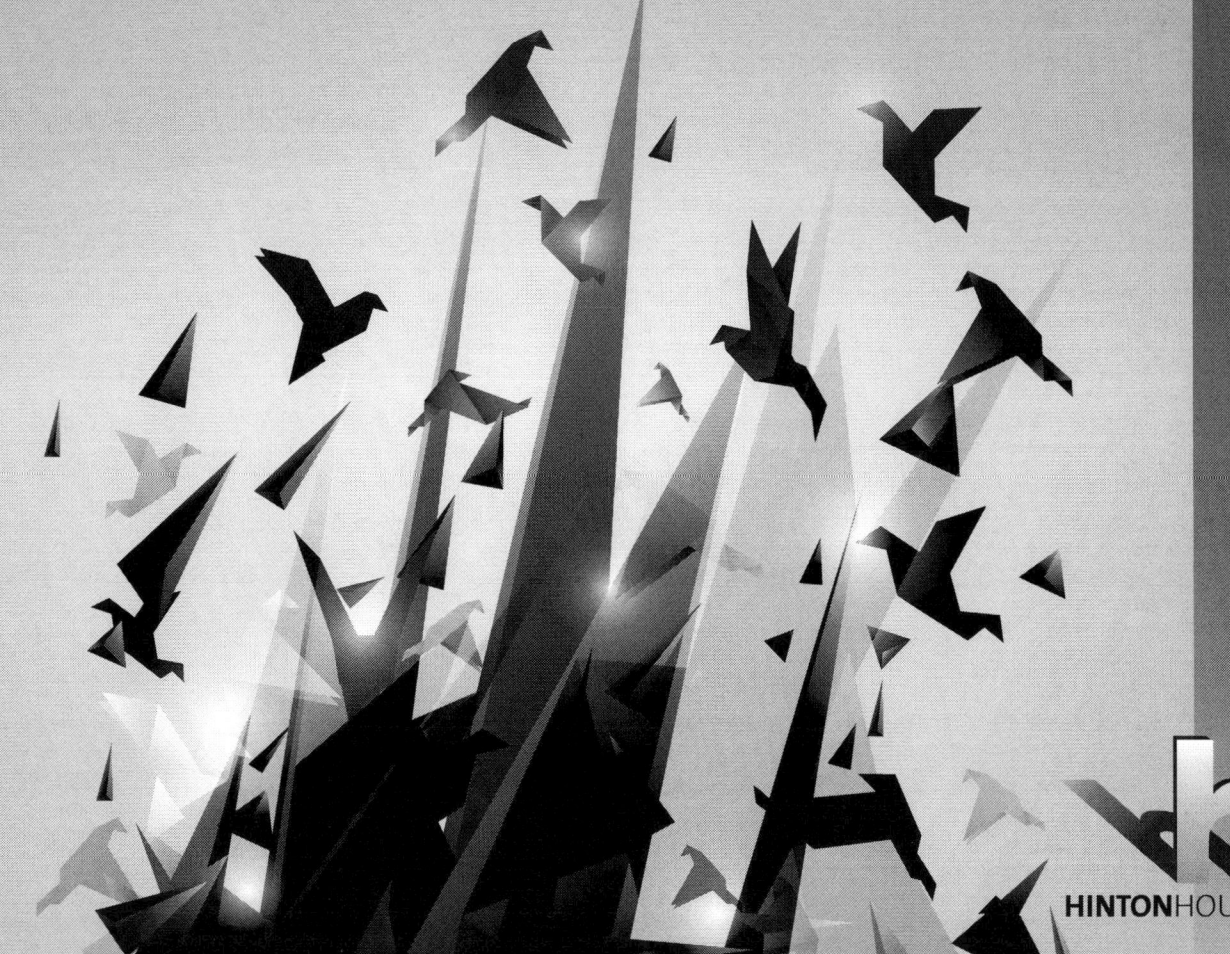

First published in 2017 by
Hinton House Publishers Ltd, Newman House, 4 High Street, Buckingham, MK18 1NT, UK
T +44 (0)1280 822557 F +44 (0)1280 822338 E info@hintonpublishers.com
www.hintonpublishers.com

© 2017 Tina Rae & Jody Walshe

Reprinted 2019, 2020

All rights reserved. The whole of this work including texts and illustrations is protected by copyright. No part of it may be copied, altered, adapted or otherwise exploited in any way without express prior permission, except in accordance with the provisions of the Copyright, Designs and Patents Act 1988 or in order to photocopy or make duplicating masters of those pages so indicated, without alteration and including copyright notices, for the express purpose of instruction and examination. No parts of this work may otherwise be loaded, stored, manipulated, reproduced, or transmitted in any form or by any means, electronic or mechanical, including photocopying or storing it in any information, storage or retrieval system, without prior written permission from the publisher, on behalf of the copyright owner.

British Library Cataloguing in Publication Data
A CIP catalogue record for this book is available from the British Library.

ISBN 978 1 906531 29 4
Printed and bound in the United Kingdom

Contents

List of Worksheets & Resources ... vii

About the Authors ... ix

Introduction: Understanding Self-Harm & Suicide ... 1

Using this Resource ... 7

Part 1 Working at the Whole-School Level ... 11
Training & Information Session for Staff and Parents & Carers ... 13
The PowerPoint Presentation Slides ... 15
Notes for PowerPoint Presentation ... 55

Part 2 Working with Groups & Individuals ... 65
1. What is Self-Harm? Myths, Realities & Tackling the Stigma ... 67
2. Understanding Stress & Anxiety ... 79
3. Triggers & Traumas: The Impact of Social Media & the Internet ... 91
4. Preventing Self-Harm & Reducing Risk: Key Tools & Strategies ... 101
5. Supporting Friends who Self-Harm: Key Issues & Sources of Support ... 111
6. Key Tools from Cognitive Behavioural Therapy (CBT) to Practise and Use ... 119
7. Using Tools from Positive Psychology to Create a More Positive Mindset ... 131
8. Breaking the Cycle & Moving Forwards ... 147

Part 3 Resources ... 157

Bibliography & References ... 181

Worksheets & Resources

Worksheets

1.1	Myths & Realities around Mental Health	73
1.2	Self-Harm Can Affect Anyone	74
1.3	Life Events that Lead People to Self-Harm	75
1.4	Myths & Realities of Self-Harm	76
2.1	The Stressors in My Life	84
3.1	Self-Harm Websites: the Debate	96
4.1	My Personal Self-Harm Prevention or Safety Plan	106
5.1	Supporting Friends who are Under Stress	115
5.2	Helping Friends who Self-Harm	116
6.1	Using Cognitive Behavioural Therapy (CBT) Skills	124
6.2	Testing the Evidence	126
6.3	Time to Reframe	127
7.1	Feeling Good & Flourishing	135
7.2	Character Strengths Information Sheet	136
7.3	My 24 Character Strengths	138
7.4	My Top Two Character Strengths: An Analysis	142
7.5	Building Resilience: Using Strengths to Cope with Problems	144
8.1	Self-Acceptance Checklist	150
8.2	When People Don't Feel Like Harming Themselves	152
8.3	My Personal Self-Harm Prevention or Safety Plan	153

Reflections Worksheets

1	Identifying My Self-Harming Behaviours	77
2	Self-Help Strategies: 'Five Looks' & Daily Stress Management Diary	87
3	My Relationship with the Internet	99
4	Getting the Mindfulness Habit	110
5	My Safety Net	117
6	Test Your Thought!	129
7	My Ten Keys to Happier Living	145
8	Course Evaluation & Feedback	155

Resources

A	Developing a Self-Harm Policy	158
B	Sample School Self-Harm Policy	162
C	Self-Harm: Information for Parents, Carers & Young People	169
D	Sample Letter to Parents & Carers Explaining the Course	172
E	Sample Letter to Young People Explaining the Course	173
F	Sources of Help, Support & Information	174
G	Information to Include in a CAMHS Referral	177
H	Initial Conversations around Self-Harm or Suicidal Thoughts with a Young Person	178

About the Authors

Dr Tina Rae has more thirty years' experience working with children, adults and families in both clinical and educational contexts within local authorities and specialist educational services. She currently works as a consultant educational and child psychologist in a range of SEBD/SEMH and mainstream contexts and for Compass Fostering as a consultant psychologist supporting foster carers, social workers and looked-after children. She is an academic and professional tutor for the Doctorate in Educational and Child Psychology at the University of East London. She is a registered member of the Health and Care Professions Council, a full member of the British Psychological Society and a member of the editorial board for the SEBDA journal *Emotional and Behavioural Difficulties* and for the *International Journal of Nurture in Education*. Tina is also a member of the SEBDA council and executive, a member of ENSEC (European Network for Social and Emotional Competence) and, until recently, a trustee of the Nurture Group Network (NGN).

Tina has published more than 75 titles on topics including well-being, attachment, emotional literacy, behavioural problems, anger and stress management, critical incidents, cognitive behavioural therapy, motivational interviewing, solution-focused brief therapy, loss and bereavement in young people, youth offending and social skills development. Among her most recent publications are *Bouncing Back & Coping with Change* (2016) and *Building Positive Thinking Habits* (2016), both from Hinton House Publishers.

Her current research is into staff well-being and resilience, including peer group supervision systems.

Tina is a regular speaker at both national and international conferences and events, and also provides training courses and supervision for school-based staff in both special and mainstream contexts and educational psychology services across the UK and internationally.

tinarae@hotmail.co.uk

Jody Walshe is an Educational Psychologist working in an outer London borough. Jody completed her doctorate in Educational and Child Psychology at the University of East London. Before commencing her training in Educational Psychology Jody worked as a teacher, learning support assistant and tutor with young people from 5–19. The focus of much of her work looked at anxiety and mental health issues in school settings.

Jody's doctoral research explored the experiences, perceptions and training needs of secondary school staff working with self-harm.

Introduction
Understanding Self-Harm & Suicide

The Context

According to the charity *Young Minds*, one in ten young people have a mental health diagnosis and one in five young adults show signs of an eating disorder. On 15 August 2015 The Observer reported that in the last ten years prescriptions for drugs used for treating ADHD have more than doubled in the UK. The issue has even garnered cross-party support in government. The UK government committed £1.4 billion over the five years from 2016 to transform children's mental health services. This is clearly essential as many families today are exposed to high levels of daily stress and the incidence of childhood depression is increasing. An estimated 10 per cent of children in any school experiences serious depression, including going through extended periods of despair and even engaging in suicidal thoughts. Young people are not enjoying carefree childhoods, but instead are coping with the devastating effects of divorce, exposure to drugs and bullying, amongst other significant stressors.

This resource aims to help promote the mental health of young people and to focus in particular upon the area of self-harm, which is undoubtedly the most challenging issue faced by professionals working with young people today. Of all the areas of mental health promotion, self-harm and suicide are probably the most challenging for both the professionals and the target groups involved. If suicide rates are to be reduced and the damage that stems from self-harm is to be ameliorated, then it is essential that these issues are addressed in a coherent manner with both those supporting these vulnerable teenagers and the young people themselves.

Self-harm is something that affects at least one in 15 young people, making their lives extremely difficult and seriously affecting their relationships with friends and family. Self-harming behaviours are almost by definition secretive, and parents and carers frequently will not know what is happening. These behaviours might involve the following:

- Taking too many tablets
- Burning
- Cutting

- Banging or scratching their own bodies
- Breaking bones
- Pulling hair
- Swallowing toxic substances or other inappropriate objects

It is important to remember that these behaviours are not done in any calculated way, as some people might think. There are many myths around self-harm; most significant is that self-harming behaviours are simply attention seeking. This is totally wrong and needs to be challenged persistently. People who self-harm do this because they are in a state of very genuine and real distress and unbearable emotional pain – self-harm is one way of releasing such pain. Some people may only self-harm on a few occasions, whilst for others it will become a regular thing – almost like an addiction. A second myth that needs to be dispelled is that young people can stop self-harming if given the right support or if simply told to do so by a significant adult. Again this is totally untrue. The behaviours are very addictive and habit forming and it is not easy to break or stop the habit without the appropriate level of support and intervention.

Who Self-Harms?

The average age for young people to begin self-harming is approximately 12 and the majority of self-harmers are aged between 11 and 25 years old. It is more common in young women than men and the majority of those who self-harm are likely to have experienced some significant physical, emotional or sexual abuse during childhood. The reasons for self-harm are many and varied, but may include the following: feelings of isolation or depression; problems in relationships with partners, friends and family; academic pressures; low self-esteem and feelings of hopelessness; sexual or physical abuse; bullying; feeling powerless – as if there is nothing that they can do to change anything in their lives; inappropriate use of alcohol or drugs; and, in very rare cases, the need to punish another person who distressed them. However, this latter reason is not the norm, as most people who self-harm are extremely private about the whole process.

Can Self-Harm be Prevented?

There are ways of preventing self-harm amongst young people and there is an increasing amount of evidence to show that this is the case. Many school initiatives, for example, anti-bullying strategies and whole-school approaches to promoting emotional health and well-being, may have an effect. These do appear to help, although there is no real evidence as yet that these initiatives have any real or long lasting impact upon self-harming behaviours. One thing that does remain a key factor for many young people who self-harm is the sense of social isolation that they experience. Self-harmers tend to think that they are the only people who engage in these behaviours – this is why educating young people around the subject and providing opportunities to gain appropriate information and increase understanding can help prevent or reduce such behaviours in both the short- and long-term. What is important is that any increased awareness is shared by parents or carers and teachers and others who come into contact with young people who self-harm. This is perhaps the key driver and rational for developing this resource.

Defining Self-Harm – An On-Going Debate

There has been a significant level of debate as to how to define self-harm. John Coleman suggests that we 'take the view that it is most helpful to consider self-harm as a continuum, ranging from behaviour which has a strong suicidal intent (e.g., some kinds of overdose) to behaviour which is intended to help the person stay alive (e.g., cutting)' (2004, p.6). Coleman adds that the problem with the term 'deliberate self-harm' is that it has an implication of wilfulness about it, which may be unhelpful to young people if they believe they have little control over their behaviour. Similarly, the problem with the term 'attempted suicide' is that some young people take an overdose with little suicidal intent (2004, p.7). 'Self-harm' therefore appears to be the best term to use in order to describe this continuum of behaviours whilst also maintaining a focus on the degree of suicidal intent.

Clearly, rates of self-harm are far more difficult to identify than those for suicide. The reasons for this are clear and obvious. In a recent study carried out by Keith Hawton for the *Samaritans*, 10.6 per cent of a sample of 4,500 secondary school pupils was found to have been involved in some form of self-harming behaviour. However, within this particular group many more had been involved in cutting (7.4 per cent) than in self-poison (3.2 per cent). The gender ratio here was approximately 3:1: in other words, more females than males were involved in this kind of behaviour. Clearly, when working with young people, any professionals involved have to be able to assess the degree of suicidal intent in such behaviours. The criteria most usefully utilised are as follows:

- The length of time that the attempt at suicide was actually being planned. If the planning period is extensive, then the risk will clearly be greater.
- The level and severity and intensity of depression that the young person is experiencing.
- The sense of hopelessness the young person is experiencing.
- If the young person was alone at the time of the self-harm incident: if the young person knows that they are not entirely alone then this would indicate a lower degree of risk.

Understanding & Preventing Self-Harm in Schools

Why Self-Harm?

There are many reasons for self-harming and there are many meanings to each of the acts perpetrated by the individuals concerned. It may well be the case that when a young person attempts to self-poison, there is a serious attempt to die. However, this attempt could also simply be a wish to escape from a terrible situation or a perceived terrible situation. It may be the only way out that the young person imagines to be possible at that point in time. He or she may also feel that they have no control over the situation and feel a total lack of self-efficacy, whilst also experiencing a sense of life being simply too much to bear or cope with. Ultimately many professionals would consider self-poisoning as a means of communication, and according to Coleman 'Concentrating on the meaning of the communication may help to prevent a repetition of the act' (2004, p.8). Coleman also makes the significant point that 'It is frequently the case that troubled relationships, either with the parent or a close friend, lie at the heart of an episode of self-poisoning. For this reason it is especially important that, following such an episode, the young person has the opportunity to talk with a caring adult, and to give expression to some of the painful emotions caused by her/his relationship difficulties' (2004, p.8).

In the same way that self-poisoning can be motivated by painful relationships and experiences, cutting and other forms of mutilation are also similarly motivated. However, it is important to point out that self-harm is at the opposite end of the continuum in terms of suicidal intent. Cutting, itself, is frequently a way or means of being able to stay alive as opposed to achieving death. Generally, forms of self-mutilation are an attempt to gain release from severe emotional tension or distress. This form of self-abuse may also be a means for the young person to redirect the anger that they feel: they may hate their abuser, but be unable to express that hatred towards the individual and this form of mutilation provides them with an outlet for these feelings.

In general, self-harm refers to a range of behaviours along a continuum ranging from low to high suicidal intent. In general, young people who tend to mutilate or cut themselves are likely to have a lower suicidal intent, while those who take an overdose may have a higher suicidal intent. What is important is that the young person accesses appropriate assessment procedures within the context of a mental health organisation. Part of this assessment would include identifying risk factors that are similar to those identified with suicide. However, risk factors for self-harm also include physical, sexual or emotional abuse, low self-esteem and anxiety and difficulties in relationships.

Suicide

Suicide rates amongst young men in the United Kingdom rose significantly during the 1980s and early 1990s. This has led to a significant amount of public attention being drawn to this topic, and rightly so, given the fact that the rates of suicide in England and Wales for young men between the ages of 15 and 24 years old rose by approximately 60 per cent within the ten year period from 1981 to 1991. This led, in 1991, to the UK Government setting a goal (Health of the Nation Strategy Document) to reduce the rate of youth suicide by 15 per cent by the end of the twentieth century. The rate was reduced by approximately 16 per 100,000 young people in 1990 to 12 per 100,000 in 2000.

In order to further support the Government's health strategy in this area, a specific 'National Suicide Prevention Strategy for England' was issued in 2002. This strategy identified six objectives, including reducing risk in key high-risk groups (for example, men) and promoting mental health well-being in the wider population, alongside reducing the availability and lethal nature of suicide methods. It still seems to be the case that young men are far more likely to commit suicide than young women. In England and Wales in the year 2000 the suicide rate was 12 per 100,000 young men, whilst it was only 4 per 100,000 young women. That is, three times as many young men as young women commit suicide every year in the UK. The UK's rate is close to that of other comparable European countries, but less than the rates in North America, Australia, New Zealand and Ireland. It is also of concern that in 2000 the rate of suicide for young men in Scotland was 36 per 100,000; in other words three times the rate in England and Wales. Regional variations of this type are of great concern, having implications for service provision and public policy.

Risk Factors

The risk factors associated with suicide can be divided between primary and secondary factors. Clearly no one young person will experience all of these factors, but is likely to experience a significant combination. Such a combination will then lead to an increased risk of suicide.

Primary risk factors include the following:

- Alcohol and drug abuse
- A sense of real hopelessness concerning the future
- Serious depression
- A previous attempt at suicide
- Some form of psychiatric disorder

Secondary risk factors include:

- A severe dent to self-esteem, which may lead to a sense of guilt or shame
- A recent loss or bereavement
- A family history of suicide
- Experiencing a significant other (e.g., a friend or significant adult) committing suicide.

Added to these factors, there are also groups of young people who are at much higher risk than would be expected within the mainstream group, including young people in custody, looked-after children, gay, lesbian or bisexual children and those who inhabit more isolated rural communities.

In Conclusion

The sessions in this programme aim to raise awareness of the risk factors for both suicide and self-harming behaviours among young people and those who care for them. As a result, attention is paid to identifying and further analysing such factors, while also attempting to improve the mental health of the young people concerned or targeted by the programme. As stated above, we are not simply concerned here with prevention of illness but also with the promotion of young people's vitality, validity, sense of self-worth and general degree of happiness. We want to really ensure that young people have the opportunity within school and other environments to experience freedom from bullying, violence and conflict and to be able to engage in their learning and social activities in an energetic, motivated and caring manner.

Using this Resource

Delivering the Programme

Keith Hawton (2015) has specifically identified the need to develop and implement preventative programmes and approaches with children and young people – both inside and outside of the school environment. This resource is designed to be used with children and young people in a wide range of settings.

This resource is divided into two parts to ensure that knowledge and skills are developed at three different levels: whole-school, group and individual levels.

Part 1: Working at the Whole-School Level

The first part is a training and information session designed to educate and raise awareness amongst parents, carers and professionals working with young people. A PowerPoint or handout-based presentation is accompanied by a group leader's script with detailed notes that relate to many of the slides. The aim is to impart much of the information provided in the Introduction to this book, alongside activities that offer the opportunity to gain a further insight into the nature of self-harm and suicide amongst young people.

In the Resources section are templates and handouts to assist you in developing a self-harm policy for your organisation or school and raising awareness amongst the whole organisation as to best practice in this area. Key aspects of the policy are addressed and a sample policy is also provided.

The Resources section also contains templates for information leaflets aimed at parents, staff and young people themselves, outlining the nature of self-harm amongst young people as well as sources of support. The intention is to dispel any myths and to ensure that accurate, up-to-date and informed facts are provided, so that any mystique and many of the fears around these issues can also be addressed.

Part 2: Working with Groups & Individuals

This section contains an eight-session programme, which can be delivered to groups of young people in a school or youth education environments. The sessions are designed to cover the main issues surrounding self-harm and suicide in young people and to provide a safe framework in which young people can develop preventative strategies and techniques, alongside recognition of the importance of peer support and appropriate access to therapeutic agencies.

The eight sessions are as follows:

Session 1: What is Self-Harm? Myths, Realities & Tackling the Stigma

Session 2: Understanding Stress & Anxiety

Session 3: Triggers & Traumas: The Impact of Social Media & the Internet

Session 4: Preventing Self-Harm & Reducing Risk. Key Tools & Strategies

Session 5: Supporting Friends who Self-Harm: Key Issues & Sources of Support

Session 6: Key Tools from Cognitive Behavioural Therapy (CBT) to Practise and Use

Session 7: Using Tools from Positive Psychology to Create a More Positive Mindset

Session 8: Breaking the Cycle & Moving Forwards

Each of the sessions includes a series of activities and clear instructions for the teacher or group leader. They all follow a similar format and are structured as follows:

Introduction

An outline of the content and key aims of the session.

Icebreaker

An icebreaker activity is used to break down any barriers and create a relaxed and empathic atmosphere within the group. Icebreakers usually take the form of a circle-time game or activity.

Activities

Practical activities to be carried out in smaller groups in order to introduce and reinforce the concepts covered in the session.

Reflections worksheet

Each of the sessions will include this opportunity to reflect and build upon the learning undertaken. This activity is intended to reinforce the concepts covered. This can be undertaken at the end of the session or as a take-home task. However, if the latter is chosen then it will be important for the group leader to go through the activity and ensure that everyone understands what they have to do and that they feel able to work on this independently of adult support or help.

Discussion & feedback

In this part of the session group members are asked to consider what they've actually learnt in the session; how they feel about their learning; how they feel about the issues covered and how they would like to proceed in the next session. For example, would they do anything differently or would they like things to be presented differently in future sessions in order to alleviate any stresses caused by the issues covered?

Important points to note

It is very important to remember that young people participating in the group activities and staff or parents and carers involved in the training session may find themselves experiencing and dealing with some very strong feelings and emotions. Self-harm and suicide clearly involve very sensitive issues. Many of the people involved in this work may have been affected by self-harming behaviours or suicidal tendencies or behaviours within their own families. Some people may currently be engaged in, or have previously engaged in, these behaviours themselves. It is therefore strongly recommended that prior to delivering the introductory training session or any work on raising awareness, and especially the group-work sessions, that you ensure adequate time is spent in enabling group members to feel relaxed and get to know each other.

Session 1 of the group work, in which the young people formulate ground rules, should be undertaken prior to delivering any of the sessions. Trust needs to be established amongst group members, regardless of which part of the programme they are working on.

It is also important for the group leader to feel skilled, knowledgeable and secure in delivering these materials and dealing with many of the strong emotions that may erupt during the course of delivery. Being trained or having access to training in this area can result in some emotional and unpredictable responses. It is recommended that where possible group leaders are trained in group work and group dynamics and also that a minimum of two facilitators deliver the training and group work. It is desirable that group leaders have access to supervision and appropriate levels of support themselves if they are to be truly effective in both delivering the key aspects of this programme and maintaining their own sense of well-being.

Part 1

Working at the Whole-School Level

Training & Information Session for Staff and Parents & Carers

Delivering the training session for parents, carers & professionals

This training session can be presented either via PowerPoint or as Handouts consisting of the PowerPoint slides. All of the material is included on the CD Rom accompanying this book. Slide 23 requires additional images of celebrities to be added. These can easily be found online.

In the course of the training session, it is important to emphasise that this is a preventative approach, although it should also enable professionals, parents and carers to provide some support to potential self-harmers and those who may already be engaging in such behaviours.

At the outset, it will be essential for the facilitator to highlight the need for such preventative work. Many parents and professionals can initially feel very concerned. This is an issue people find extremely challenging and difficult to talk about. Many would simply like it to go away and feel that raising the issues around this topic will trigger self-harming behaviours in young people – almost creating a self-harm epidemic. This is, of course, not true and Hawton (2015) makes this abundantly clear.

The statistics around mental health problems in young people and the significant increase in recent years also provide support for such preventative work. Talking about self-harm does not trigger young people – it helps to demystify the topic and allows them to develop self-management strategies and an awareness of how to access help and support that is appropriate and useful to them. Who do young people generally talk to and disclose to first? It is usually a close friend. This is why this topic needs to be on the curriculum in every school and also presented in a range of other learning and support contexts that young people engage with. They need to develop their skills in managing anxiety and stress and to understand that self-harm is not an answer. It is an addictive behaviour that ultimately needs to be replaced by more effective and less harmful ways of managing pain and anxiety. It is hoped that this programme goes some way to achieving such objectives.

The training session should take approximately an hour and a half to deliver and is suitable to be delivered to parents, carers, teachers, youth leaders and other adults and professionals working with young people in a range of contexts. It is recommended that the training groups are kept relatively small and that the session is repeated within larger settings as required. Numbers of up to approximately 30 seem to be most appropriate and easy to facilitate. The sensitive nature of this topic does, however, mean that the facilitator(s) will need to carefully consider their approaches and have some skills in terms of managing groups, while also themselves being aware of the key issues, self-help strategies and preventative tools that children and young people may make use of. Tackling and understanding the myths around this topic are imperative and an in-depth awareness of the issues is to be encouraged. This may well require some additional reading and preparation but, naturally, we would presume that trainers would undertake this level of preparation.

The PowerPoint or Handout presentation is supported by detailed notes where the slides seem to demand this, so should be relatively easy to work through. Attention and care will be needed, however, should any participant have experience of these issues on a more personal level and this would need to be highlighted at the start of the session. If someone does feel vulnerable or upset by the content at any point, then of course they should be able to withdraw, but the training facilitators should also ensure that such individuals can access some debriefing at the end of the session if they so require it.

UNDERSTANDING & PREVENTING SELF-HARM
An introduction for staff, parents & carers

TINA RAE

JODY WALSHE

Slide 1

Aims of this presentation

- To review the definition and meaning of the term 'deliberate self-harm' and its prevalence among young people.
- To highlight the ways in which school-based staff can and should be able to talk to young people about these problems.
- To discuss when to refer on to other professional services.
- To highlight some evidence-based approaches and strategies for use in schools, including strategies from Cognitive Behavioural Therapy (CBT) and Motivational Interviewing (MI) to manage stress and anxiety in young people as a preventative strategy.
- To highlight the need to monitor online activity.
- To outline the contents of the programme for young people.
- To provide time to discuss any issues group members may have.

Slide 2

Understanding & Preventing Self-Harm in Schools

Training & Information Session

Slide 3

All of these celebrities are known to have harmed themselves.

- Sid Vicious
- Pete Doherty
- Princess Diana
- Marilyn Manson
- Demi Lovato
- Cara Delevigne

Slide 4

**QUICK QUIZ
True or False?**

- People who self-harm are attention seeking.
- People who self-harm use it as a way of releasing pressure and feelings.
- It is easy to stop self-harming.
- People who self-harm are usually feeling suicidal.
- People who self-harm typically hide it from others.
- Self-harm is a cry for help.
- Self-harm is more common among girls than boys.

What is 'deliberate self-harm'?

- The act of deliberately causing harm to oneself either by causing a physical injury, by putting oneself in dangerous situations and/or self neglect.
- Intentional self-poisoning or injury, irrespective of the apparent purpose of the act. (NICE, 2004)

Slide 5

Self-harm:
An act of religious devotion

Slide 6

Understanding & Preventing Self-Harm in Schools

Self-harm: a form of protest

BBC NEWS UK EDITION

Shias stage anti-US protest
Protests against the US presence in Iraq have been staged by Shias in the city of Karbala at the climax of a pilgrimage that has attracted one million people. Groups of marchers chanted slogans against a US-imposed government calling for unity among Shias. Many hit their backs with flails or cut their heads with swords in ritual self-flagellation.

Slide 7

Self-harm: a way of restoring health!

Slide 8

Young Minds 'Talking Self-Harm' report

- 2,461 online interviews were conducted in August 2012
- 1,002 young people (aged between 14 and 24)
- 265 secondary teachers
- 994 parents of children between 11 and 24
- 200 GPs

Slide 9

'Self-harm among young people is the **number one issue** that young people themselves are concerned about among their peers, in a list that includes gangs, bullying, drug use and binge drinking.'

Slide 10

So?

- Why is this issue not openly discussed and presented as part of the curriculum in every school across the country?
- You tell me ... discuss and feedback.

Slide 11

- Self-harm is the issue that all groups feel least comfortable approaching with young people.
- Two in three teachers, parents and young people think that they would say the wrong thing if someone turned to them.

Slide 12

Slide 13

Self- harm?

Some well-known figures, e.g., Sophie Dahl, have undergone extreme weight-loss – could this be described as self-harm?

Understanding & Preventing Self-Harm in Schools © Tina Rae & Jody Walshe 2017

Slide 14

Did you know?

- Girls as young as five years old are worried about the way they look and their size.
- One in four 7 year-old girls have tried to lose weight at least once.
- Between one-third and a half of young girls fear becoming fat and engage in dieting or binge eating.
- Over half of girls (and a quarter of boys) think their peers have body image problems.
- Children and young people with body image dissatisfaction are less likely to engage in learning and participation in school.

Understanding & Preventing Self-Harm in Schools © Tina Rae & Jody Walshe 2017

Slide 15: Did you know?

- Thousands of young British men and boys are injecting themselves with anabolic steroids – once the preserve of cheating athletes – in the quest for a muscular physique.
- Steroids are a controlled Class C drug – possession isn't illegal but supplying them is – so it is difficult to ascertain exact usage figures.
- NICE estimates that almost 60,000 people aged 16-59 used steroids in England and Wales in 2013.
- Side effects of steroids – high blood pressure, cardiovascular damage, hair loss, fusion of bones, heart attack, stroke, over growth of forehead, severe acne, and Psychosis.

Slide 16: And more ...

- Vanity is now also the 'curse' of boys.
- They are bombarded with 'aspirational' body images, e.g., David Beckham's underwear ads, men's health covers, film and reality TV stars with 6 packs
- Can you get that look without steroids?
- 'Yeah, but it would take ten years whereas I can do it in two.'
- 'The bigger you are in the gym the more respect you get.'
- 'You get more girls when you're muscly than when you're skinny.'

We can see evidence of self-harm in news items on a daily basis.

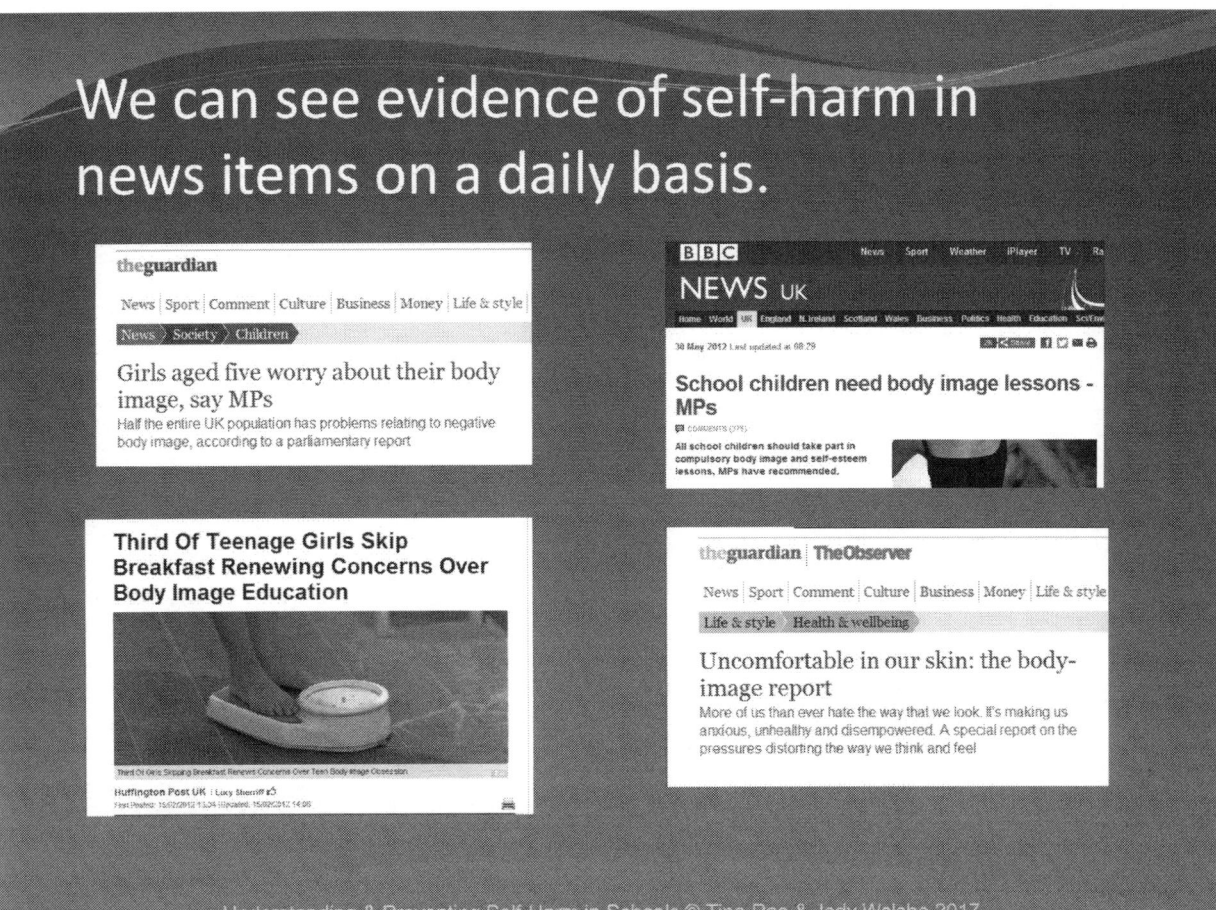

Slide 17

Social context for both genders

- Pressure to grow up too fast, too soon.
- Sexualisation of both genders and the implications of this for well-being.
- Physical and emotional disconnection.
- Advertising which plays on pseudo-adultness.
- '2016 Girl's Attitudes Survey' by Girlguiding.

47% of 11-21 year-olds feel their looks hold them back.
69% of 7-21 year-olds feel they are not good enough.

Slide 18

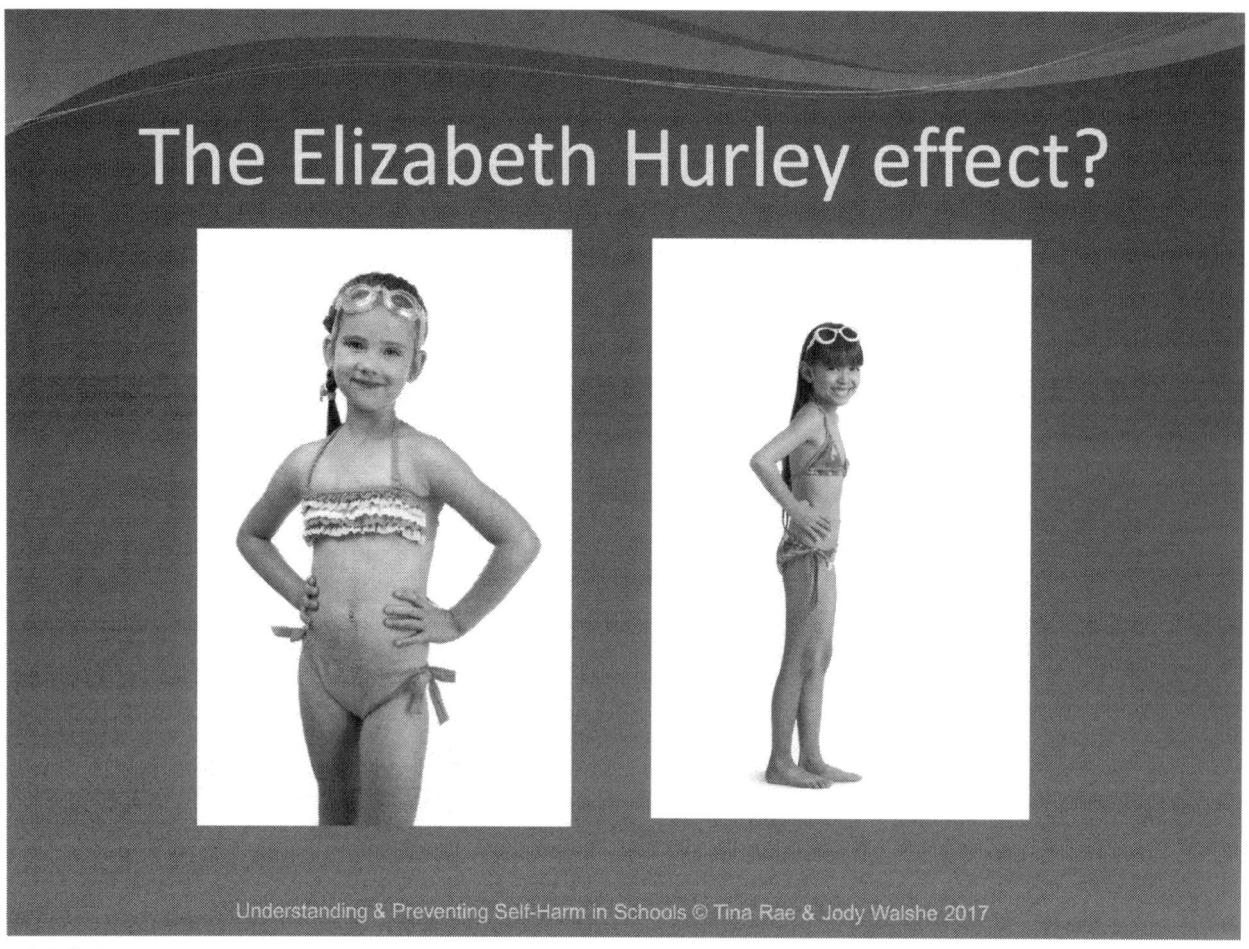

Understanding & Preventing Self-Harm in Schools

The Elizabeth Hurley effect?

Slide 19

A hyper-vigilant generation?

Slide 20

Slide 21

Risk factors for self-harm

Behaviour
- Fat teasing
- Body checking
- Diets
- 'Bad' foods
- Body loathing

Physical
- Severe weight loss/fluctuating weight
- Cold
- Thinning hair
- Teeth
- Restless
- Exercising
- Food avoidance

Slide 22

Starting to discuss self-harm in schools

- Use the 'right' examples...
- Let's talk about the issues...

Understanding & Preventing Self-Harm in Schools

> Media images of celebrities are often airbrushed or Photoshopped. What comes to mind when you see these pairs of images?

Slide 23

There are two Barbie dolls sold every second somewhere in the world.

The target market for Barbie doll sales is young girls aged 3 to 12 years.

If Barbie were an actual women, she would be 5'9" tall, have a 39" bust, an 18" waist, 33" hips and a size 3 shoe!

At 5'9" tall and weighing 110lbs, Barbie would have a BMI of 16.24 and fit the weight criteria for anorexia. She likely would not menstruate.

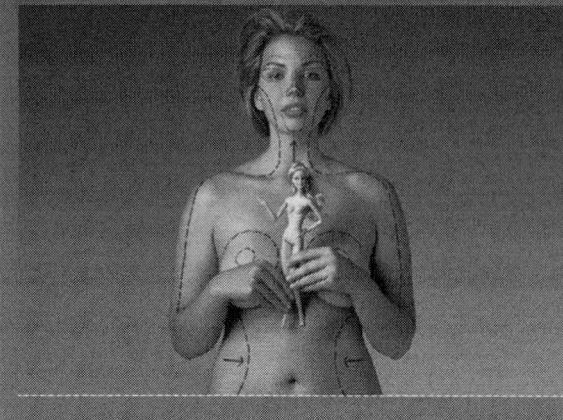

If Barbie was a real woman, she'd have to walk on all fours due to her proportions.

Slide 24

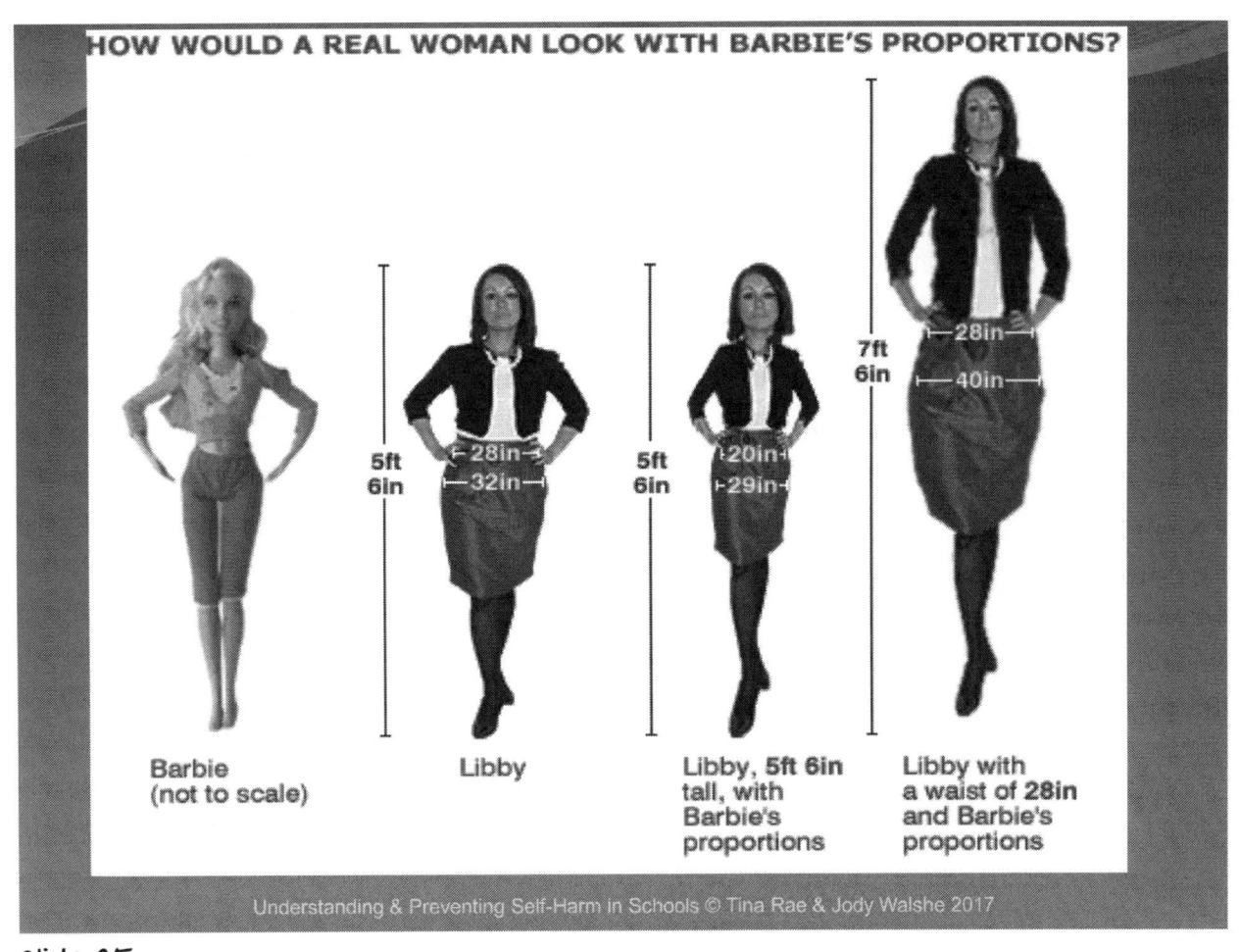

PowerPoint Slides

Slide 25

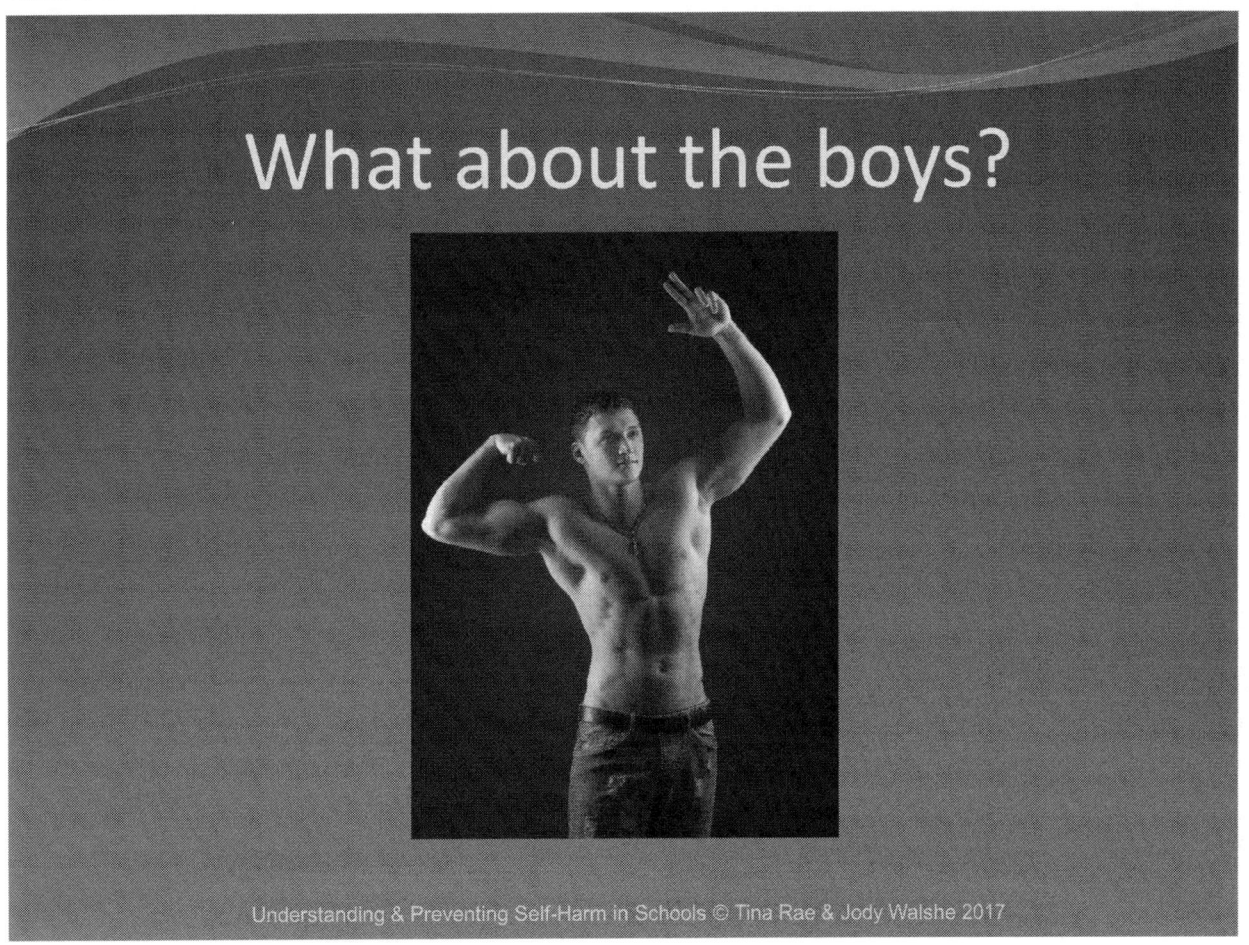

HOW WOULD A REAL WOMAN LOOK WITH BARBIE'S PROPORTIONS?

| Barbie (not to scale) | Libby — 5ft 6in, 28in/32in | Libby, 5ft 6in tall, with Barbie's proportions — 20in/29in | Libby with a waist of 28in and Barbie's proportions — 7ft 6in, 28in/40in |

Understanding & Preventing Self-Harm in Schools © Tina Rae & Jody Walshe 2017

Slide 26

What about the boys?

Understanding & Preventing Self-Harm in Schools © Tina Rae & Jody Walshe 2017

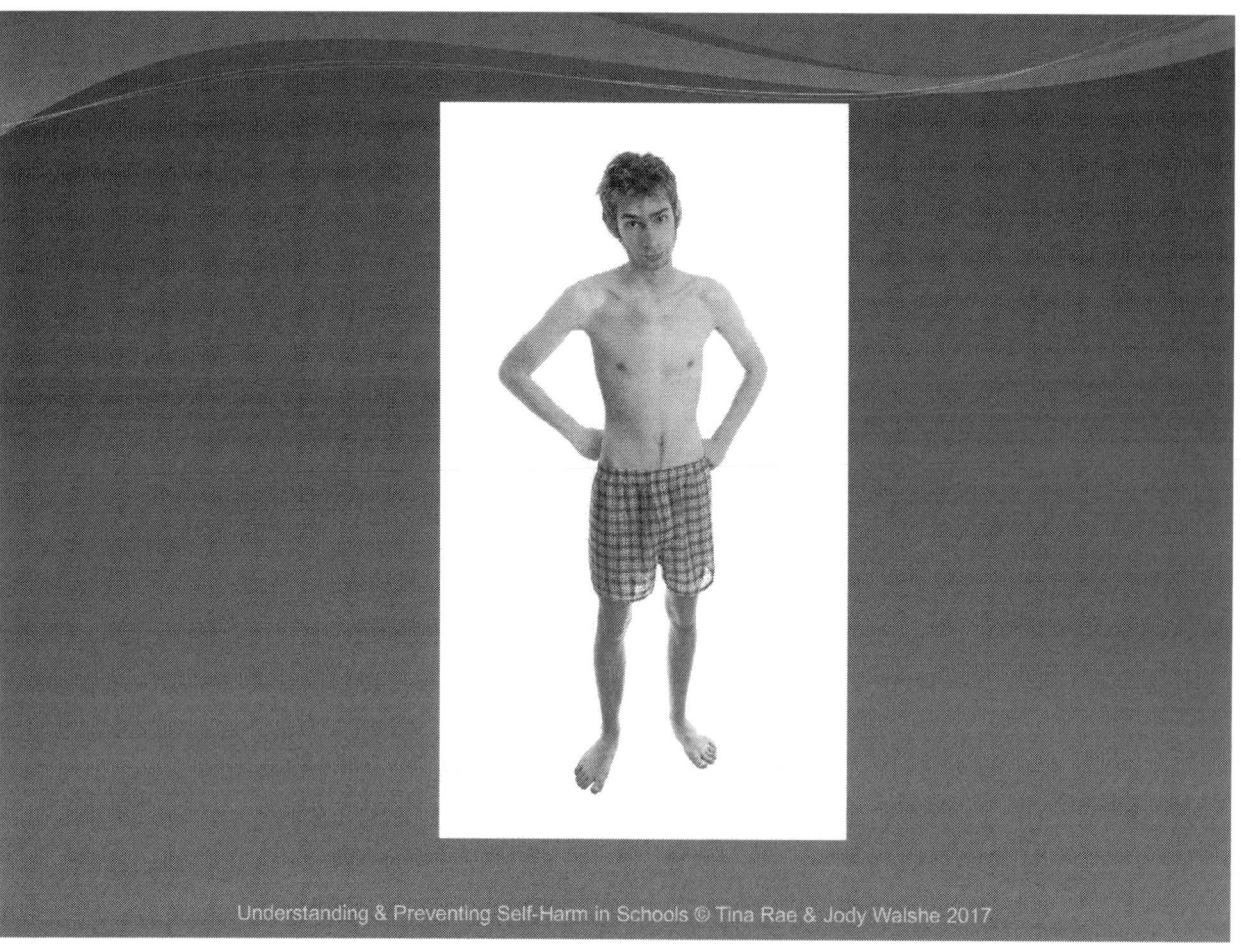

Understanding & Preventing Self-Harm in Schools

Slide 27

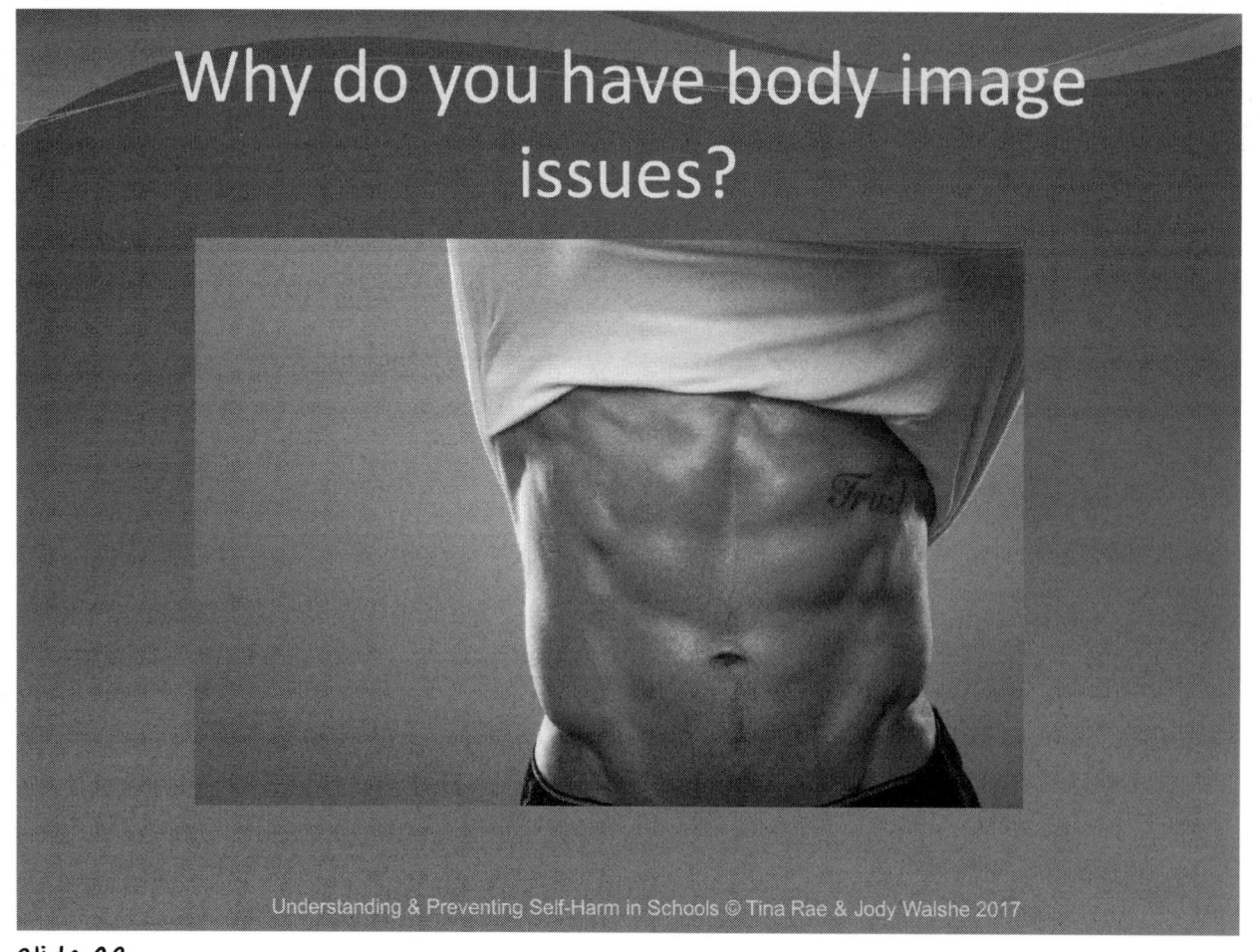

Why do you have body image issues?

Slide 28

The boys' Barbie?

- GI Joe
- Action Man
- Action and Super Heroes
- Computer game characters
- Covers of 'men's health' magazines

Slide 29

What have we done to young people? The real traumas?

- Anorexia: a serious mental health condition
- Wannarexia: 'wannabe annorexic'
- Bigorexia: muscle dysmorphia or reverse anorexia

Slide 30

NSPCC'S 2015 SURVEY

- 700 young people surveyed aged 12 and 13.
- 1 in 10 were worried they were addicted to porn.
- More than 1 in 10 had made/been part of sexually explicit video.
- Peter Liver (Director of Child Line) reports that children have said watching porn makes them feel depressed, gives them body image problems and they feel pressured to engage in sexual acts they are not ready for.
- A report from the charity Childwise (92013/4) – revealed the website Pornhub was among the top 5 favourite sites for boys aged 11 from 16.

Slide 31

Dame Kelly Holmes

- Double Olympic gold medallist
- Cut her wrists and chest
- Slashed her body with scissors
- Hid her self-harming from those close to her

Slide 32

Dame Kelly Holmes

- '... in constant agony from a damaged calf and tissue strain, leaving me unable to run properly'
- 'intolerable mental pressure'
- 'plunged into despair after a series of injuries left me fearing I would never reach my potential'
- 'I made one cut for every day I'd been injured'

- 'With each cut I felt I was punishing myself but at the same time I felt a sense of relief that drove me to do it again and again'
- 'I knew deep inside that I wouldn't go any further'
- 'The whole episode was nothing more than a cry of despair
- 'It's the lowest I have ever been'

Slide 33

Where to start?

- Myths
- Realities

Slide 34

Understanding & Preventing Self-Harm in Schools

Young people may be more likely to self-harm if they feel:

- that people don't listen to them
- hopeless
- Isolated and alone
- out of control
- powerless – it feels as though there's nothing they can do to change anything

Slide 35

What to do?
Advice for staff on the ground in school...

Slide 36

If a young person discloses self-harm:

First and foremost, try to **remain calm** (even if you don't feel calm).

KEEP CALM AND CARRY ON

Slide 37

- If his or her wounds are fairly minor, provide basic, appropriate first aid, and a dose of 'tender love and care'.

- If the wounds are deeper, or won't stop bleeding, they should be seen by a health-care professional.

- You may need to take the young person to casualty or, if necessary, call an ambulance.

Slide 38

Slide 39

- Strive to be **accepting** and **open-minded**. Provide an ear to listen, a shoulder to cry on, a hand to hold, and focus on the person not the self-harm behaviour.

- Young people who self-harm can find it very hard to talk about what has happened and are often afraid of how people will react.

- The reaction a young person receives when they disclose their self-harm can have a critical influence on whether they go on to access supportive services.

Slide 40

- Talk to them when they feel like self-harming. Try to understand their feelings, and then move the conversation onto other things.

- Take some of the mystery out of self-harm by helping them find out about self-harm perhaps by using the internet or the local library.

- Offer to assist them in seeking professional help, e.g., a GP or counsellor but avoid taking control - many young people who self-harm struggle with control issues.

- Help them to think about their self-harm not as a shameful secret, but as a problem to be sorted out.

- Assure them that it's okay to talk about their need to self-harm, and reassure them that they have your support even if you don't understand why they are doing it or what they are going through.

- Be mindful that any indication of a negative emotion or being judgemental is likely to aggravate the situation.

Slide 41

Emotional Awareness & Resilience

- Learning to cope better with the emotions associated with self-harm can help reduce or stop it.
- Educate young people about the emotional states that can lead to self-harm, and those that increase coping and resilience.
- Resilience is 'the happy knack of being able to bungee jump through the pitfalls of life'.
- Teaching emotional awareness and literacy creates a platform for raising the topic of self-harm in context, i.e. as part of the curriculum. This is likely to be more palatable for teachers, parents and young people.

Slide 42

Slide 43

- Build up to educating around self-harm in context, e.g., learning to recognise a range of difficult emotions (anger, stress, pressure etc.), and discuss positive and negative coping mechanisms.

- Lessons that build resilience have the power to simultaneously minimise the number of young people who start to self-harm and de-stigmatise those that do, helping them to feel less isolated and more able to access appropriate support.

Slide 44

What *not* to do!

Don't…

- Try to be a therapist – therapy is complicated and you have enough to deal with as the young person's teacher, friend, or relative.

- React strongly, with anger, hurt, or upset - this is likely to make them feel worse. Talk honestly about the effect it has on you, but do this calmly and in a way that shows how much you care for them.

- Expect them to stop overnight – it's difficult and takes time and effort.

Slide 45

Don't…

- Try not to take it as a personal affront if the young person says they cannot talk to you about it.

- Avoid giving ultimatums; e.g., 'stop or else …' as they rarely work, and may escalate the situation.

- It is important that the decision to stop comes from the person themselves.

Slide 46

Don't...

- Struggle with them when they are about to self-harm – it's better to walk away and to suggest they come and talk about it rather than do it.

- Make them promise not to do it again.

- Say that you won't talk to them unless they stop self-harming.

Slide 47

Summary

- There is no right or wrong way to respond ... and this is what makes it hard for us!

- **DON'T**: Ignore it, get angry, stop talking to a young person or demand that they stop.

- **DO**: Ask them how they're feeling, let them know you'll be there for them, talk when they are ready to talk, help them get professional help.

Slide 48

Online Issues

Many young people feel a sense of isolation ... there is a need for vigilance on social media.

Don't forget the battle is ongoing.

Does social media fulfil a need for contact and affirmation?

Slide 49

Online Impact

- One in five school children with a history of self-harm and eating disorders questioned by researchers at Oxford and Stirling Universities said *they first learnt about it after seeing or reading something online,* second only to hearing about it from friends.

- The Royal College of Psychiatrists says it is now 'seriously concerned' about the growing number of websites that glamorise the problem or show gory images of cuts and scars.

Slide 50

Daily access...

Slide 51

What the Research Tells Us...

- Research indicates that the Internet may represent a preferred medium for otherwise isolated children and young people to communicate with others - namely, others who self-injure.

- One part of the Internet's appeal stems from the anonymous nature of the interaction it provides; indeed, research indicates that anonymous e-communication may hold particular appeal for those who experience psychological distress and other emotional difficulties - many of the risk factors associated with self-harm and eating disorders.

Slide 52

PowerPoint Slides

Self-harm websites made me do this...

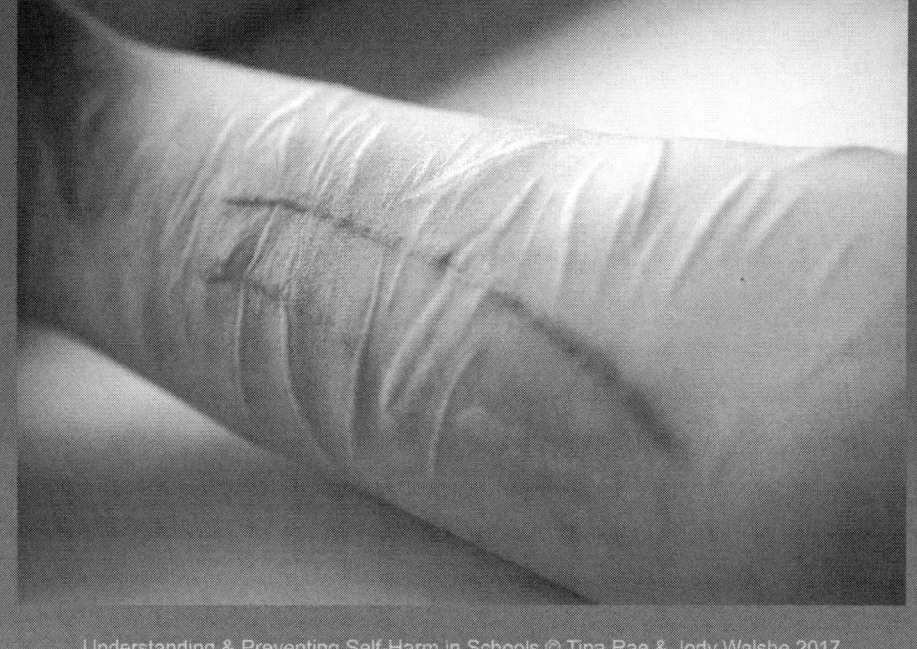

Slide 53

Welcome to my site, says the 14-year-old girl behind 'Depression and Disorders'

Slide 54

I need this blog because... you don't understand

Slide 55

'It helps me', says one 14-year old

- 'Nobody knows I have this blog. It helps me. Tumblr is powerful because it shows that you're not alone. You can see that you're not the only one who's struggling.'
- 'But it's bad too because my Tumblr dashboard can be really triggering sometimes with all the posts from others.'
- 'Like if you self-harm and you see pictures of cuts/scars it can be very triggering. It can make you start self-harming too. It encourages me to cut.'

Slide 56

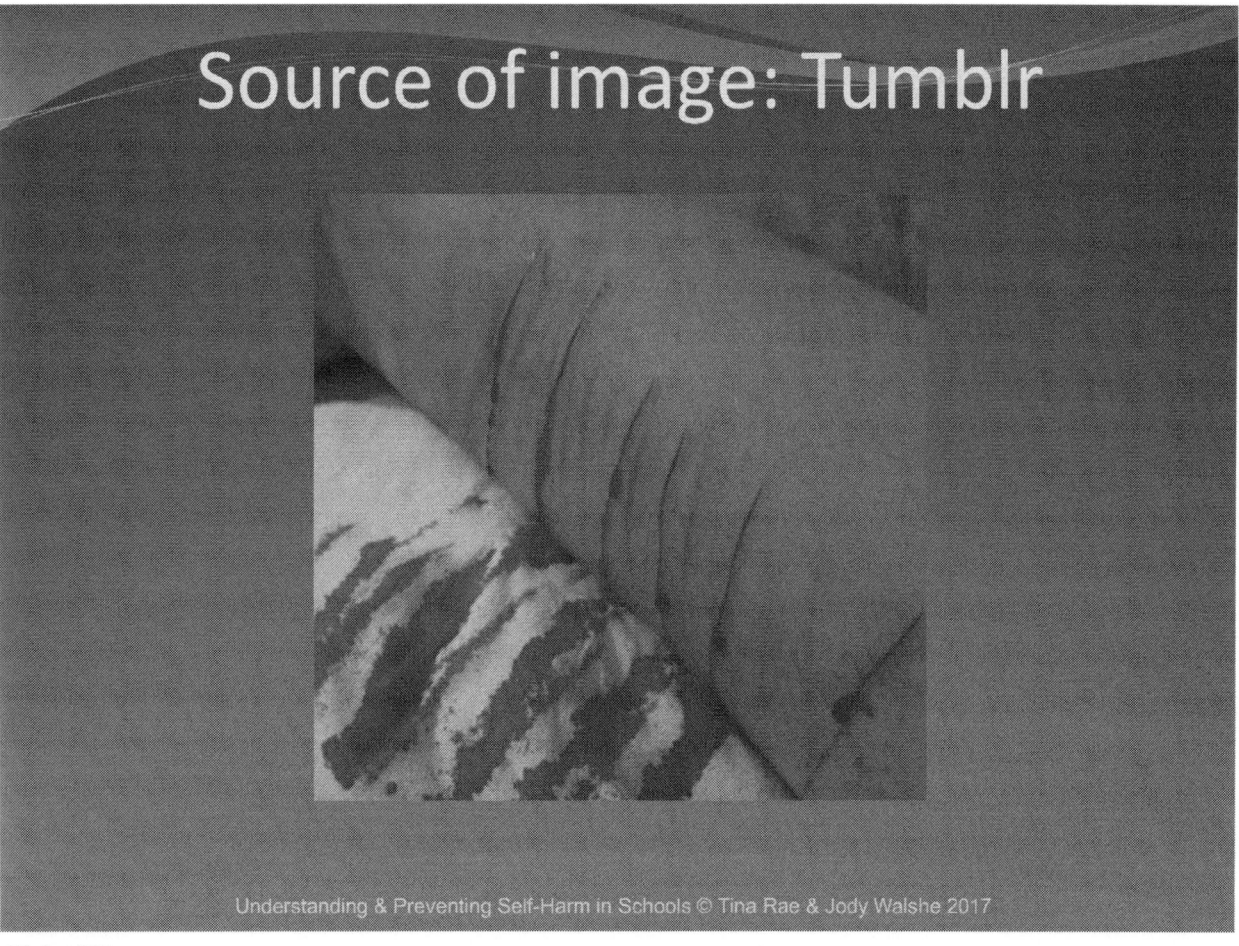

Source of image: Tumblr

Slide 57

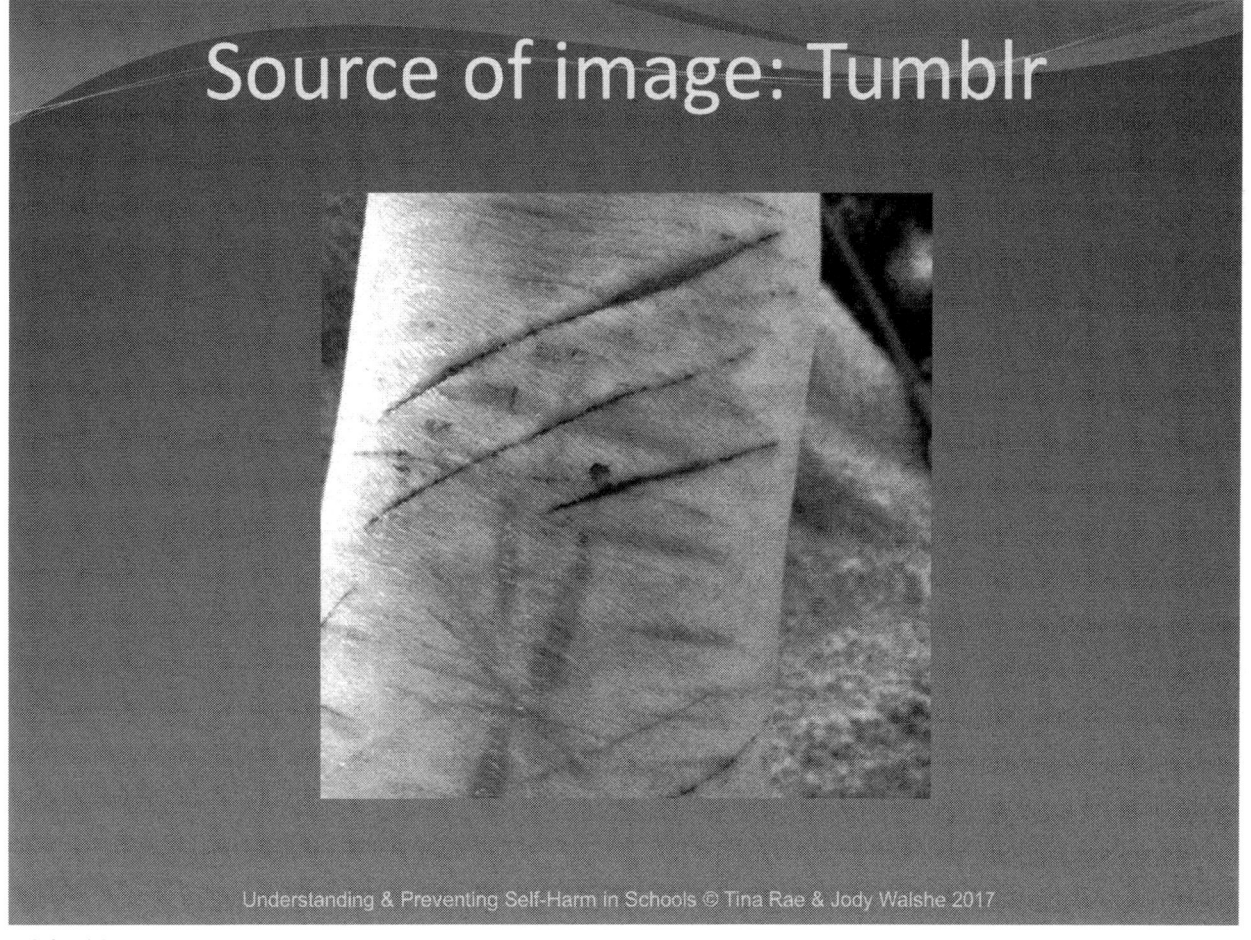

Source of image: Tumblr

Slide 58

Understanding & Preventing Self-Harm in Schools

Source of image: Tumblr

I HATE MY THIGHS

Slide 59

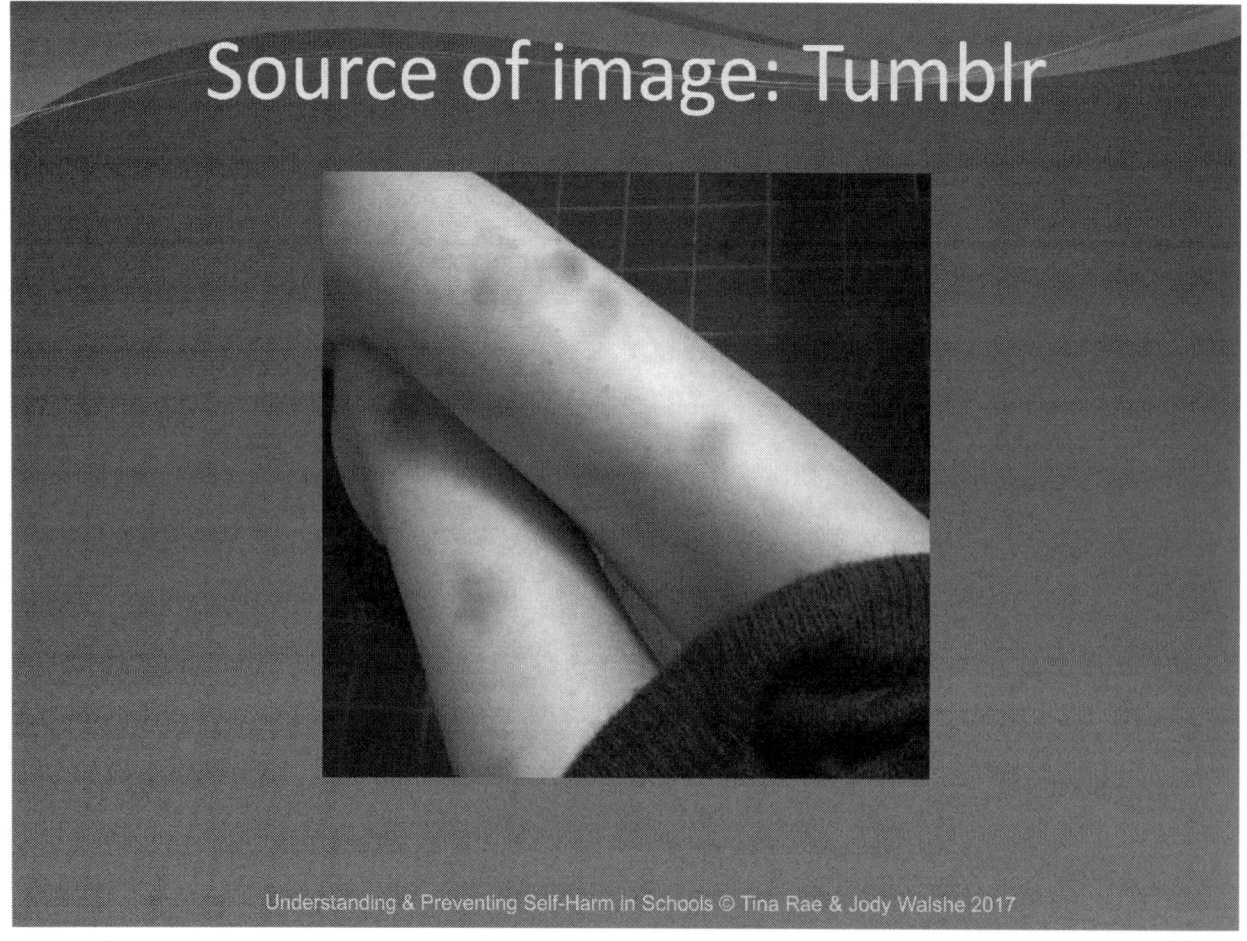

Source of image: Tumblr

Slide 60

PowerPoint Slides

Source of image: Tumblr

Cut deeper.

Understanding & Preventing Self-Harm in Schools © Tina Rae & Jody Walshe 2017

Slide 61

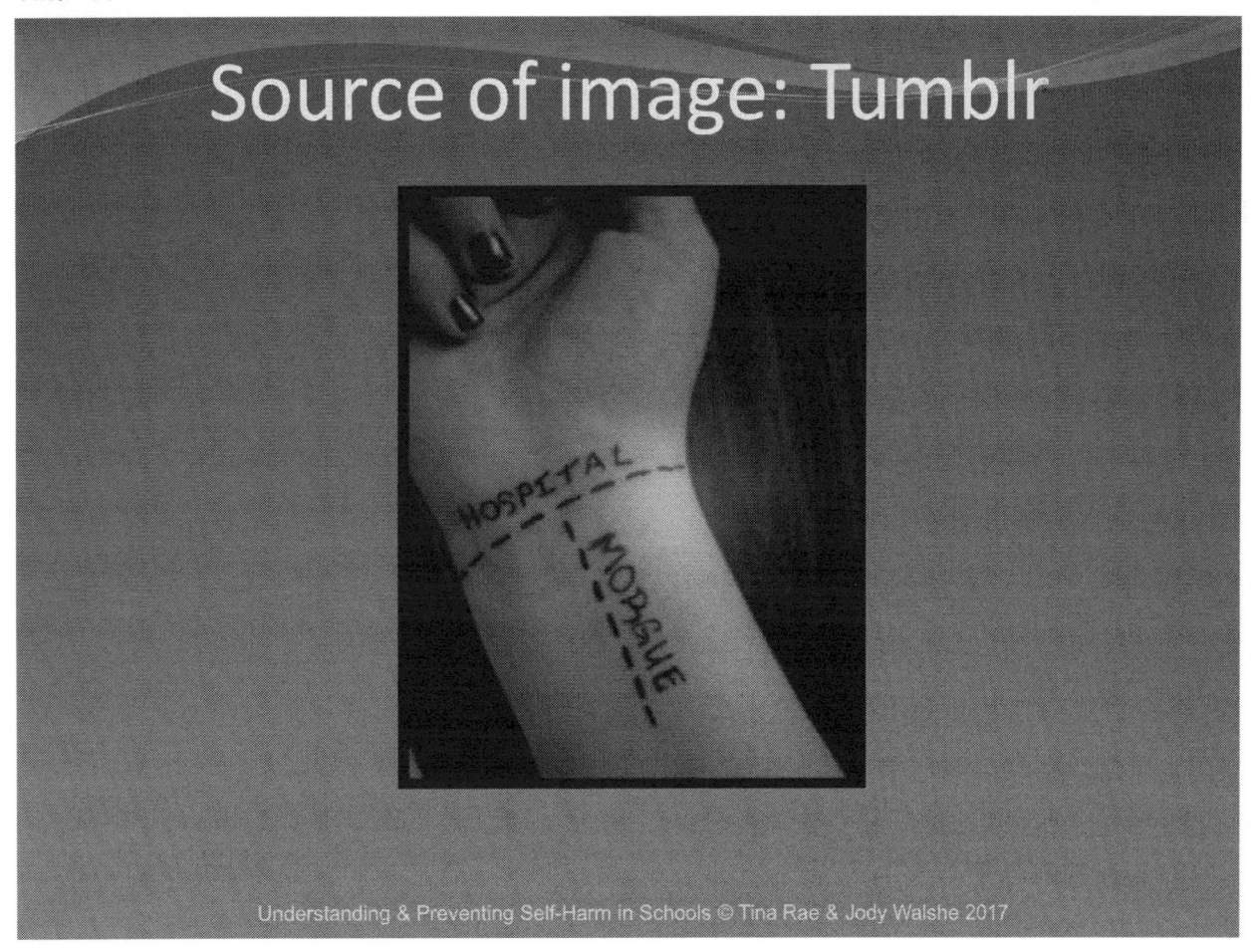

Source of image: Tumblr

Understanding & Preventing Self-Harm in Schools © Tina Rae & Jody Walshe 2017

Slide 62

Training & Information Session

Misguided?

'[Tumblr] hasn't [contacted me about my blog violating their guidelines]. I'm not really worried about it. If they really force me to stop, I'll start a new blog, because I really need a blog like this, it helps me. I understand why sites are trying to censor it because we don't want more people to have those disorders, but on the other hand: it helps the people who are already suffering.'

Slide 63

Stop and Reflect...

- At this point in the presentation what do you think? Helpful or unhelpful or both?
- Discuss with a partner and feed back to the group.

Slide 64

DO NOT FORGET!

- Who do children and young people usually *talk* to *first* if they are self-harming?
- What are the implications of this for preventative work in schools?
- What does the research tell us?
- What can staff *do* in schools in terms of prevention?

Slide 65

The Sessions in this Programme

- 1 What is Self-Harm? Myths, Realities & Tackling the Stigma
- 2 Understanding Stress & Anxiety
- 3 Triggers & Traumas: The Impact of Social Media & the Internet
- 4 Preventing Self-Harm: Key Tools & Strategies
- 5 Supporting Friends who Self-Harm: Key Issues & Sources of Support
- 6 Key Tools from Cognitive Behaviour Therapy (CBT) to Practise and Use
- 7 Using Tools from Positive Psychology to Create a More Positive Mindset
- 8 Breaking the Cycle & Moving Forwards

Slide 66

When to Refer to CAMHS

- If you are concerned about a young persons emotional state then it is advisable to refer to CAMHS.
- You will need to discuss this with the young person and agree that their parents will need to be involved.
- If in doubt telephone CAMHS for a consultation.

Slide 67

Developing a Self-Harm Policy
The Purpose of the Policy

- Clear guidelines and procedures.
- Include means of raising self-esteem and emotional literacy.
- Information on support systems for those who are dealing with students who self-harm.
- See Sample School Self-Harm Policy n this resource for suggested content including roles and responsibilities and ground rules.

Slide 68

Handouts

- Information Leaflet for Parents, Carers & Young People
- Developing a School Self-Harm Policy
- Sample School Self-Harm Policy

Slide 69

Prevention is better than cure...

Logical Conclusions
- Provide copious opportunities to learn and practise a range of effective stress management and study skills.
- Increase young people's ability to cope with stress.
- Maintain locus of control and well-being.
- Educate young people in the areas of deliberate self-harm and eating disorders, where and how to get help, how to become more autonomous and less at risk.

Slide 70

Teach ALL Students Methods of Coping with Stress & Anxiety

- Diet
- Relaxation
- Meditation
- Time management
- Physical exercise
- Additional training
- Counselling
- Reframing
- Improving social support networks
- Peer support groups
- Improved resource allocation
- Self-analysis

Slide 71

Principles of Motivational Interviewing (Miller & Rollnick)

- Express empathy with patient's perceptions

- Develop discrepancy between present behavior & personal goals.

- Avoid argumentation and defensiveness.

- Redefine, rather than confront, resistance.

- Support self-efficacy through autonomy support.

Slide 72

In Summary

- This issue will not go away and will go 'underground' if the online sites are made illegal.
- We need to understand how this all works and the effects on young people.
- We need to let them know *how much* we know and dispel the mystery ... *let's talk* sessions in school and at home?
- We need to use appropriate tools to monitor and assess the online behaviours and activities of self-harmers and those with eating disorders.
- We need to direct (as appropriate) young people to those sites and sources of information which we know to be helpful.
- VIGILANCE IS KEY.

Slide 73

WE ARE NOT SUICIDAL!
It keeps us calm, please understand.

Slide 74

References

Kress V.E. & Hoffman R.M., 2008, 'Non-suicidal self-injury and motivational interviewing: Enhancing readiness for change', *J Ment Health Couns*, 30 (Suppl 4):311-329.

Lenhart A. & Madden M., 2007, *Social networking websites and teens: An overview*, Pew Internet & American Life Project, Washington DC.

Lewis S.P. & Baker T.G., 2011, 'The possible risks of self-injury web sites: a content analysis', *Arch Suicide Res*, 15(Suppl 4):390-396.

Lewis S.P., Heath N.L., St Denis J. & Noble R., 2011, 'The scope of nonsuicidal self-injury on YouTube', *Pediatrics*, 127(Suppl 3):e552-e557.

Slide 75

References

Miller W.R. & Rollnick S., 1991, *Motivational interviewing: Preparing people to change addictive behavior.* Guildford Press, New York.

Mitchell K. & Ybarra M., 2007, 'Online behavior of youth who engage in self-harm provides clues for preventive intervention', *Preventive Medicine: An International Journal Devoted To Practice And Theory*, 45(Suppl 5):392-396.

Rideout V., Foehr U.G. & Roberts D.F., 2010, *Generation M2: Media in the Lives of 8- to 18-Year-Olds*, Kaiser Family Foundation, Menlo Park

Slide 76

References

Rodham K., Gavin J. & Miles M., 2007, 'I hear, I listen and I care: a qualitative investigation into the function of a self-harm message board', *Suicide Life Threat Behav* 2007, 37(Suppl 4):422-430.

Sornberger M.J., Heath N.L. & Lewis S.P., 2011, *The Digital Butterfly Effect: Knowledge Transfer and NSSI Research*, New York.

Whitlock J., Purington A. & Gershkovich M., 2009, 'Media, the internet, and nonsuicidal self-injury', American Psychological Association, 139-155.

Resources: www.b-eat.co.uk

Slide 77

Further reading
All Party Parliamentary Group Report - Reflections on Body Image
http://joswinson.org.uk/en/document/appg-on-body-image-report

American Psychological Association – Task force report on the Sexualisation of Girls
http://www.apa.org/pi/women/programs/girls/report.aspx#

Department for Education - Letting Children be Children
https://www.education.gov.uk/publications/eOrderingDownload/Bailey%20Review.pdf

Media Industry research – Pretty as a Picture
http://www.credos.org.uk/write/Documents/Pretty%20as%20a%20picture%20Dec%202011.pdf

Media literacy programmes/resources
http://www.mediasmart.org.uk/frontpage (sections for children, parents and teachers)
http://mediasmarts.ca/
http://www.dove.co.uk/en/Our-Mission/Self-Esteem-Toolkit-and-Resources/default.aspx (reading for parents/mentors, self-esteem activities for use at home/school)
http://www.bbc.co.uk/learningzone/clips/body-image-and-the-media/5496.html (video clip for teaching activities)
http://www.mypopstudio.com/ (website for pupil's to explore different media)
http://www.apa.org/pi/women/programs/girls/report.aspx# (links to further media literacy resources)

Slide 78

Understanding & Preventing Self-Harm in Schools

> Thank you for listening and participating!
>
> Understanding & Preventing Self-Harm in Schools © Tina Rae & Jody Walshe 2017

Slide 79

Notes for PowerPoint presentation

The following notes are designed to facilitate discussion during the PowerPoint presentation. Slides which are clearly in need of further clarification or information from the presenter are taken in turn.

Slide 3

Self-harm affects men and women at different points in their lives. All of these celebrities have been known to have harmed themselves.

Images of the following can be found online, and used to illustrate this slide. Sid Vicious – Pete Doherty – Princess Diana – Marilyn Manson – Demi Lovato – Cara Delevigne

Cara Delevigne, in an interview in 2015, said:

> *I was hit with a massive wave of depression and anxiety and self-hatred, where the feelings were so painful I would slam my head against a tree to knock myself out. I never cut, but I'd scratch myself to the point of bleeding. I just wanted to dematerialise and have someone sweep me away.*

Demi Lovato told ABC news:

> *It was a way of expressing my own shame, of myself, on my own body ... I was matching the inside to the outside. And there were some times where my emotions were just so built up, I didn't know what to do. The only way that I could get instant gratification was through an immediate release on myself.*

She attended therapy and says that the support she received has changed her life.

Princess Diana:

> *You have so much pain inside yourself that you try and hurt yourself on the outside because you want help, but it's the wrong help you're asking for. People see it as crying wolf or attention seeking ... I just hurt my arms and my legs; and I work in environments now where I see women doing similar things and I'm able to understand completely where they're coming from.*

Sid Vicious harmed himself when performing on stage.

Manson has previously talked about self-harm, telling *Spin Magazine* in 2009:

> *My lowest point was Christmas Day 2008, because I didn't speak to my family ... I was struggling to deal with being alone and being forsaken and being betrayed by putting your trust in one person, and making the mistake of that being the wrong person. And that's a*

mistake that everyone can relate to. I made the mistake of trying to, desperately, grasp on and save that and own it. And every time I called her that day — I called 158 times — I took a razor blade and I cut myself on my face or on my hands.

Pete Doherty harmed himself while being filmed for a BBC documentary in 2005. The BBC decided not to broadcast the footage.

Slide 4

Discuss in the group the following statements before revealing the answers below.

People who self-harm are attention seeking – **FALSE** – If attention was the reason for self-harming there are far less painful and degrading ways of getting it. It is important to think of self-harm as attention *needing* rather than attention seeking.

People who self-harm use it as a way of releasing pressure and feelings – **TRUE** – The reason for self-harming will be different for every individual

It is easy to stop self-harming – **FALSE** – Self-harm needs to be understood in the context of what it means for the young person who does it. Often it is a way of coping with difficult emotions or distracting yourself, which is habit-forming – meaning that young people can come to rely on it.

People who self-harm are usually feeling suicidal – **FALSE** - It is often thought that self-harm is linked to suicide and this worries people a great deal. But the vast majority of young people who self-harm are not trying to kill themselves – they are trying to cope with difficult feelings and circumstances – for many it is a way of staying alive. Many people who commit suicide have self-harmed in the past and this is one of the many reasons that self-harm must be taken very seriously.

People who self-harm typically hide it from others – **TRUE** - Self-harm is usually carried out in private. Much of the self-harming that occurs goes undiscovered. Many of those who self-harm go to great lengths to make sure it goes undiscovered.

Self-harm is a cry for help – **FALSE** – Self-harm is very private and personal for most young people. Young people often go to great lengths to cover up their injuries under clothes, make-up or with excuses. The attention self-harm does bring for young people is often negative.

Self-harm is more common among girls than boys – **FALSE** - Recent research shows that there is less difference in the rates of self-injury between men and women than previously thought.

Slide 5

Discuss among the group the definitions of 'deliberate self-harm'. Self-harming behaviours are almost by definition secretive and parents and carers frequently will not know what is happening. These behaviours might involve the following:

- Taking too many tablets
- Burning
- Cutting
- Banging or scratching their own bodies
- Breaking bones
- Pulling hair
- Swallowing toxic substances or other inappropriate objects

Slide 11

Take 5 minutes in groups of two to three people to discuss this question and then feedback to the whole group.

Slide 14

Body image dissatisfaction can lead to a lack of confidence, participation and motivation and therefore withdrawal from social interactions.

Slide 15

Body image is not a 'girl issue' – the facts show that young men are under enormous pressure and going to drastic and dangerous lengths to look muscular.

Slide 17

We know there is a problem, and so how do we begin to tackle it?

Slide 18

Girlguiding's 2016 Girl's Attitudes Survey explored opinions of 1,600 girls and young women aged 7 to 21.

This report shows that for today's girls concern over appearance and body image emerges at an ever-younger age. Girls linked appearance with popularity, happiness and success. Fear that people will criticise their body stops girls from wearing clothes they like (53% 11–16 year-olds), taking part in sport/exercise (41% 11–16 year-olds), or speaking up in class (39% 11–16 year-olds).

Slide 23

Select images of well-known people in which they have clearly been airbrushed and compare with more natural images of the same person. Note down pairs of words that come to mind when you see these images.

Slide 24

Images around girls present a narrow view of what the ideal image is for women.

Slumber Party Barbie was introduced in 1965 and came with a bathroom scale permanently set at 110lbs and a book entitled *How to Lose Weight*: the directions inside stated simply 'Don't eat'.

We start to recognise ourselves in the mirror from around the age of two. Girls of age five are worried about their weight and appearance, so girls only experience a couple of years when they don't have these worries.

Slide 25

A real woman with Barbie's proportions is a physical impossibility. It is important to stop and reflect on how unrealistic many female images are.

Slide 26

Body image issues are not just 'girl' issues.

Slide 27

Quickly note down what kind of images of masculinity are presented in the media.

Slide 28

Media images of masculinity present a very generic picture of what a 'real' man looks like.

- Extremely muscular
- Big build
- Tall

Slide 29

Where do these pressures come from for boys?

This powerful image of masculinity that involves ideals of height, weight and muscle can be linked to G.I. Joe, introduced to the public in 1964 – the male equivalent of Barbie. Extremely muscular and bulky action heroes, super heroes and video game characters present a physically impossible ideal for boy. When looking at the covers of men's 'health' magazines, boys and young men are presented with unrealistic, airbrushed and digitally altered images.

Slide 30

With all of these pressures on young people what is the result? Body dysmorphia comes in many different forms and presents in both men and women.

- **Anorexia nervosa** – is a serious mental health condition. It is an eating disorder in which people keep their body weight as low as possible.
- **'Wannarexia'** – 'wannabe anorexic' – a label applied to someone who claims to have anorexia or wishes they did, but does not. 'Wannarexics' may be inspired or motivated by the pro-anorexia, or 'pro-ana' community that promotes or supports anorexia. In online communities this is often used as a pejorative term.
- **Muscle dysmorphia** ('bigorexia', or 'reverse anorexia') is a mental health issue that is characterised by a fear of being too small, and perceiving oneself as small and weak even when one is actually muscular and large.

Slide 32

To illustrate this slide you could select and add an image of Dame Kelly Holmes with her olympic medals, looking fit and healthy.

Slide 34

When we start thinking about mental health in general and self-harm in particular, there are lots of myths that create stigma around these issues. These myths make it harder for young people to reach out, and understanding the realities helps us to be able to support them.

The Myth	The Reality
People who self-harm are attention seeking.	If attention is the reason for self-harming, there are far less painful and degrading ways of getting it. It is important to think of self-harm as attention *needing* rather than attention seeking.
People who self-harm are manipulative.	Self-harm is usually carried out in private. Much of the self-harming that occurs goes undiscovered. Many of those who self-harm go to great lengths to make sure it goes undiscovered.
Self-harmers need to see a psychiatrist in order to get better.	Psychiatry alone has had little success helping those who self-harm.
People who self-harm tend to be teenage girls and they grow out of it.	Recent research shows that there is less difference in the rates of self-injury between men and women than previously thought and there is no evidence that people 'grow out of it'.
People who talk about suicide do not mean to do it.	People who talk about suicide may be reaching out for help. Very many people contemplating suicide are experiencing anxiety, hopelessness and depression and may feel they have no other option. The experience of the *Samaritans* shows that many people who take their lives have given warning of their intentions in the weeks prior.
Self-harm is when you cut yourself.	There are many forms of self-harm, of which cutting is one. Others include scratching, self-hitting, self-poisoning, burning and head banging.
Young people self-harm to fit in with their peer group.	Self-harm is a response to emotional distress. Young people do not self-harm to fit in.
Self-harm is a rite of passage.	Self-harm is never just the usual part of adolescence. Young people self-harm.
Taking about suicide encourages it.	Rather than encouraging the behaviour, talking openly can give the individual other options and time to rethink their decision.
If the injury isn't that bad – the problem can't be that bad.	Severity of emotional distress is not linked to the severity of the injury. It takes courage for someone to say that they have self-harmed and this must be taken seriously, regardless of how severe (or not) the injury is.

Slide 36

At this point we are going to think about practical ways in which school staff can support young people.

Slide 37

Staying calm when a young person discloses self-harm is incredibly important, since if they are met with understanding it can have a critical influence on whether they will then go on to access support services.

It is important to remember that it takes great courage for a young person to talk about their self-harm.

Evidence shows that young people face overwhelming negative responses when they disclose self-harm.

This can be emotional or stressful for us as professionals.

Slide 39

Whenever we are having a conversation with a young person about a sensitive and difficult topic such as self-harm, it is helpful to provide a clear idea of how long you have available and what the conversation might be like, so that they know what to expect.

Slide 42

Emotional awareness and resilience are valuable qualities for all young people, not just those experiencing emotional distress. A whole-school approach to developing these protective factors is important and makes it easier to raise topics like self-harm with staff, parents and young people.

http://www.cellogroup.com/pdfs/talking_self_harm.pdf
Cello plc is a health-focused insight and strategic marketing group and in partnership with teen mental health charity, *YoungMinds*, it conducted a piece of ground-breaking, year-long research in 2012. It included advanced qualitative research, professional online community forums and social media discourse research, integrated with a nationally representative quantitative sample of 2,461 people. It explores society's perceptions of young people who self-harm and the barriers that exist between providing the help they so clearly need.

Key findings:

- 'There is a desire for more conversation and action to help young people. The majority of people believe that they need to be able to offer support to young people who self-harm but nobody feels empowered to act.'
- 'Currently, there is little open communication and considerable scope for stigma and fear. Parents associate a young person self-harming with failed parenting and shame; many are frightened to let the issue "out of the home" [and] over a third say they would not seek professional help.'
- Teachers feel helpless and unsure as to what they can say; 80 per cent want clear practical advice and materials that they can share directly with young people.
- Ninety-seven per cent of young people believe that self-harm should be addressed in schools, with two in three feeling that it should be part of lessons. Greater teaching around emotional awareness and literacy appears a strong and obvious platform for raising the topic of self-harm in context.

Slide 43

Developing emotional awareness and resilience helps to empower young people and de-stigmatise mental health issues. There is still a lot of stigma around mental health issues, which can make those who are suffering feel even more isolated.

Slide 45

It can be emotional when talking to a young person about their self-harm; make sure that you remember that it is very difficult to stop self-harming and, if a young person feels that by continuing to self-harm they will disappoint or anger you (a person they trust enough to talk to about their self-harm), this could just make them feel worse and even more isolated.

Slide 46

Ultimatums – not only do they hardly ever work, but they just put further pressure on an already overwhelmed young person.

Slide 47

Forcing the young person to make promises to stop or withholding affection/contact until they do, will leave the young person feeling even worse and alone. Hard as it may feel, they have trusted you with a difficult and upsetting piece of information and these actions may make the young person feel shame about their self-harm. Many young people who have disclosed self-harm talk about getting negative responses, such as being told they are *selfish*.

Slide 49

The role of social media – we may not feel familiar with it, but we need to build our knowledge so that we are informed to support young people.

Slide 53

Polling commissioned in the run up to Self-Harm Awareness Day in 2015 (1 March 2015) has shed light on the alarming number of 11- to 21-year-olds exposed to online self-harm images. Organised by the leading UK youth charities *ChildLine, selfharmUK, YoungMinds* and *YouthNet*, the research found that a significant number of young people 'felt like hurting themselves' in response to such images.

The polling also revealed the scale of young people self-harming in the UK today. Over half of 11- to 14-year-olds have either self-harmed themselves or know someone who has self-harmed, whilst eight out of every ten 18- to 21-year-olds say they have self-harmed or know someone who has self-harmed.

Key findings:

- One in every four 11- to 14-year-olds and seven out of ten 18- to 21-year-olds said they had seen images online showing someone self-harming.
- Of those who had seen an image of someone self-harming, over half of all 11- to 14-year-olds and one in every four 18- to 21-year-olds said they had 'felt like hurting themselves' after seeing these images.
- Of those who had seen an image of someone self-harming, nine out of every ten 11- to 14-year-olds and eight out of every ten 18- to 21-year-olds said they had found the images upsetting.
- Of those who had seen an image of someone self-harming, six out of every ten 11- to 14-year-olds and one in ten 18- to 21-year-olds said they had shared images of someone self-harming on social media.
- Over half of all 11- to 21-year-olds said they wouldn't know how to report an image of someone self-harming on social media.
- Around a third of 11- to 18-year-olds and 69 per cent of 18- to 21-year-olds said they would go online for support and information about self-harm.

Part 2

Working with Groups & Individuals

Session 1
What is Self-Harm? Myths, Realities & Tackling the Stigma

Introduction

Preparation – Before you start

In this initial session you will be introducing the topic of self-harm to the group of young people. As this is a very sensitive and complex topic, it is vital that you take the time to understand how such behaviours develop, the prevalence of these behaviours and the different ways of supporting young people – both at a preventative and intervention level.

The following information may be of use in terms of clarifying some of the issues. Self-harm remains a major public health issue amongst young people in the United Kingdom and it is something that affects at least one in 15 young people, making their lives extremely difficult and seriously affecting their relationships with friends and family. Self-harming behaviours are almost by definition secretive and parents and carers frequently will not know what is happening. These might involve young people doing the following:

- Taking too many tablets
- Burning
- Cutting
- Banging or scratching their own bodies
- Breaking bones
- Pulling hair
- Swallowing toxic substances or other inappropriate objects

It is important to remember that these behaviours are not done in any calculated way, as some people might think. There are many myths around self-harm, most significantly the belief that such behaviours are simply attention seeking. This is totally wrong and needs to be challenged persistently. People who self-harm do so because they are in a state of very genuine and real distress and unbearable emotional pain – self-harm is one way of releasing such pain. Some people may only self-harm on a few occasions, while for others it will become a regular thing – almost like an addiction. A second myth that needs to be dispelled is that young people can stop self-harming if given the right support or if simply told to do so by a significant adult. Again this is completely untrue. If it were that easy to stop, then these young people would certainly cease their self-harming behaviours.

The average age for young people to begin self-harming is approximately 12-years-old and the majority of self-harmers are aged between 11- and 25-years-old. It is more common in young women than men and the majority of those who self-harm are likely to have experienced some significant physical, emotional or sexual abuse during childhood (Hawton, 2015).

The reasons for self-harm are many and varied but may include the following:

- Feelings of isolation or depression
- Problems in relationships with partners, friends and family
- Academic pressures
- Low self-esteem and feelings of hopelessness
- Sexual or physical abuse
- Bullying
- Feeling powerless and as if there's nothing that they can do to change anything in their lives
- Inappropriate use of alcohol or drugs
- In very rare cases, the need to punish another person who has distressed the young person; however, this is not the norm as most people are extremely private about the whole process.

There are ways of preventing self-harm amongst young people and there is an increasing amount of evidence to show that this is the case (Hawton, 2015). A key factor for many young people is the sense of social isolation that they experience. Self-harmers tend to think that they are the only people who engage in these behaviours – this is why educating young people in this subject and providing opportunities to gain appropriate information and increase understanding can help prevent or reduce such behaviours in both the short and long-term. What is important is that any increased awareness is shared by parents or carers and teachers and others who come into contact with young people who self-harm.

In this initial session you will introduce the topic and provide the group with opportunities to reflect upon the stigma around mental ill-health and some of the myths about self-harm. They will also be able to consider some of the life events that may be a cause or contributory factor. At the outset, it is vital to set up a context or environment that protects the safety and security of all involved. You will need to have liaised with other colleagues to ensure that any vulnerable students, or those who are already engaging in such behaviours, are provided with the appropriate support from the outset. Briefing of both school staff and parents/carers will ideally have been undertaken via the training session provided in Part 1 of this book, and the group members will also have been briefed by means of a letter outlining the aims of the sessions (see Resource E: Letter to Young People Explaining the Course).

The students should be encouraged to discuss any initial concerns at this point, prior to the delivery of the sessions, so that effective support systems can be put into place. You should begin by briefly summarising the content of the course and give the group the opportunity to voice any concerns they may have. You should also ensure that students are prepared for the fact that they may find some aspects of the course difficult.

Group rules

It is strongly recommended that you give the group the opportunity to discuss and create a series of group rules at the very start of the first session. This should enable the boundaries to be clearly identified and will help to guaranty an appropriately confidential and supportive atmosphere within the group. Establishing rules for the group is essential in order to ensure a caring and supportive learning environment throughout this programme. It is important that these rules are negotiated among the group members themselves in order that they have ownership of them. You will have suggestions and ideas as to what the rules might contain, but it is more preferable that you steer the students towards these during their discussion rather than dictating to them.

The rules should advise the group about what to do rather than what *not* to do, for example: 'We will listen to others' opinions.' As the discussion takes place, write the agreed rules on the whiteboard or a flipchart. They can then be typed up and a copy given to each student at the start of the next session. You could also display the rules on a poster in the classroom.

Each member of the group can then sign their own copy of the group rules to demonstrate their commitment to following the rules. Throughout the forthcoming sessions there may be times when students fail to follow the rules. At these times you should encourage the students to correct each other in a respectful manner, perhaps referring to the rule that has been broken, rather than always being the person who reprimands the group.

The following suggestions may be helpful in creating your rules:

- What is said in the room, stays in the room.
- We will respect each other's opinion; there will be no 'put downs'.
- We will listen when someone else is talking and wait our turn to speak.
- We will show no prejudice regardless of race, religion or sexual orientation.
- We will share at our own comfort level and not speak for others.
- We will try to participate to the best of our ability and encourage others.

Understanding & Preventing Self-Harm in Schools

Icebreaker: Mental Health – the Stigma

Many people experience problems with their mental health or well-being at some point in their lives. Unfortunately, there remains an enormous stigma around these issues for many people. Prior to considering who self-harms and why, it is important to highlight some of the myths around mental health in particular.

Initiate a discussion among the group by giving each person a copy of Worksheet 1.1, 'Myths & Realities Around Mental Health', and reading aloud the myths regarding mental health. The students can discuss each myth in turn and identify their own views and feelings regarding each one in the list. Ensure that before moving on to the next myth you explain the corresponding reality to the group.

The second part of this icebreaker highlights a range of individuals who say they have engaged in self-harming behaviours. This is in no way intended to glamorise the issues, but instead should demonstrate to the group that the levels of unhappiness and anxiety that lead to such behaviours can be experienced by anyone – regardless of fame or social or economic circumstances.

Give each group member a copy of Worksheet 1.2, 'Self-Harm Can Affect Anyone', and ask them first to try and identify the individuals. Then ask them to see if they can match the correct quotation of description to the people. Once everyone has done so, discuss in the group the different reasons that people might self-harm.

Answers:

1–F   Pete Doherty harmed himself while being filmed for a BBC documentary in 2005. The BBC decided not to broadcast the footage.

2–E   Sid Vicious harmed himself when performing on stage.

3–D   Princess Diana said in a BBC interview: 'You have so much pain inside yourself that you try and hurt yourself on the outside because you want help, but it's the wrong help you're asking for. People see it as crying wolf or attention seeking ... I just hurt my arms and my legs; and I work in environments now where I see women doing similar things and I'm able to understand completely where they're coming from.'

4–C   Marilyn Manson has previously talked about self-harm, telling *Spin Magazine* in 2009, 'My lowest point was Christmas Day 2008, because I didn't speak to my family ... I was struggling to deal with being alone and being forsaken and being betrayed by putting your trust in one person, and making the mistake of that being the wrong person. And that's a mistake that everyone can relate to. I made the mistake of trying to, desperately, grasp on and save that and own it. And every time I called her that day — I called 158 times — I took a razor blade and I cut myself on my face or on my hands.'

5–B   Demi Lovato told ABC news: 'It was a way of expressing my own shame, of myself, on my own body ... I was matching the inside to the outside. And there were some times where my emotions were just so built up, I didn't know what to do. The only way that I could get instant gratification was through an immediate release on myself.' She attended therapy and says that the support she received has changed her life.

6-A Cara Delevigne, in an interview in 2015 said: 'I was hit with a massive wave of depression and anxiety and self-hatred, where the feelings were so painful I would slam my head against a tree to knock myself out. I never cut, but I'd scratch myself to the point of bleeding. I just wanted to dematerialise and have someone sweep me away.'

Activities

1.1 Life events that lead young people to self-harm

Prior to the session make copies of Worksheet 1.3, 'Life Events that Lead People to Self-Harm', and cut each into ten separate cards. Divide the students into groups of four and give each group a set of 10 cards. Each card shows a life event that may lead to a young person to self-harming behaviours.

Ask the small groups to discuss each event in turn and then place the cards in order, running from what they believe is the *least* likely to lead to self-harming to the *most* likely. Where possible the members of each group should reach agreement through discussion and debating with each other.

Once they have completed the activity the groups can feedback their ranking order to the rest of the group. Encourage each group to justify their ideas and the ranking order given and highlight any similarities and differences in their responses. You can then reveal actual order (as based on Hawton's survey for the *Samaritans*, 2003).

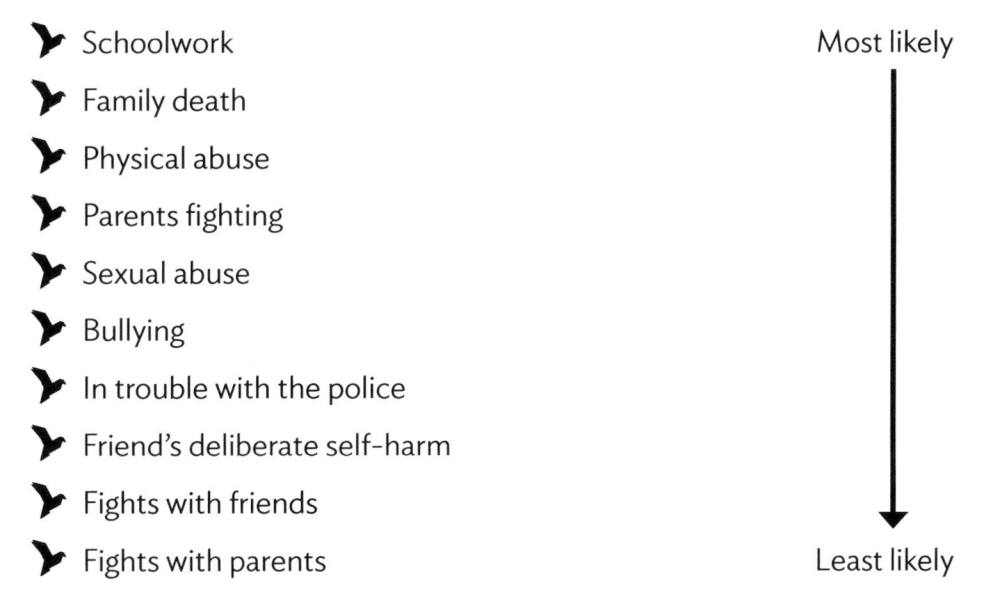

- Schoolwork
- Family death
- Physical abuse
- Parents fighting
- Sexual abuse
- Bullying
- In trouble with the police
- Friend's deliberate self-harm
- Fights with friends
- Fights with parents

Most likely ↓ Least likely

1.2 Myths and realities of self-harm

This activity aims to explore the group's perceptions of self-harm and to create a safe environment to challenge myths and misunderstandings. Give each person a copy of Worksheet 1.4, 'Myths & Realities of Self-Harm', and encourage the group to engage in a discussion about the different myths and the corresponding realities. Read out the myths to the group one at a time, and ensure that you have fully explained the reality before moving on to the next myth.

Reflections Worksheet

Use the reflections activity to reinforce the concepts you have covered in the session. Give each person a copy of Reflections Worksheet 1, 'Identifying My Self-Harming Behaviours'. Explain that we all do things that may be harmful to ourselves at different levels. Ask the group to think about what these might be and to complete the worksheet.

This worksheet can either be used in the session as a reinforcement activity or as a take-home task.

Discussion & Feedback

Ask the group to reflect on what they have learnt during the session. Some key points and questions to include in the discussion are as follows:

- What do we understand by the term 'self-harm'?
- Why do we think people engage in self-harm?
- Many people will encounter someone in their lives who self-harms or attempts suicide and some people in the group may have already had such experiences. We may have confused feelings when those we love or care about are involved and it is good to talk about those feelings.
- We must not judge people who do self-harm or attempt suicide, but look to help and support them and try to identify better ways of coping with difficult times in our lives.
- We also need to be able to dispel the myths around self harm.

Worksheet 1.1
Myths & Realities Around Mental Health

Statement	Myth or Reality	Explanation
Mental health problems are rare.	MYTH	Mental health problems affect one in four people in any one year. So even if you don't have a mental health problem, it's likely your best friend, a family member or work colleague will be affected.
People with mental health problems are often violent.	MYTH	People with mental health problems are much more likely to be the victims of violence. This myth makes it harder for people to talk openly about mental health problems. It can also make friends reluctant to stay in touch.
People can't work if they have a mental health problem.	MYTH	With one in four people affected by mental health problems, you or someone you know probably works with someone with a mental health problem.
People with mental health problems never recover.	MYTH	Many people can and do recover completely from mental health problems. Alongside professional help, the support of friends and family, as well as getting back to work, are all important in helping people recover.
Other people can't tell if you have a mental health problem.	REALITY	Mental health problems are as real as a broken arm, although there isn't a sling or plaster cast to show for it. Many of those who are affected deal with it alone, because nobody else knows.
On average, people who experience mental health problems don't live as long.	REALITY	However, it's not the mental health problem that's responsible. The physical health needs of people with mental health problems are often dismissed, causing higher rates of death from heart attacks, diabetes and cancer for people with severe mental illness.
We all have mental health, like we all have physical health.	REALITY	Just like our physical health, our mental health will vary from time to time and it is important that we take care of both.
People with mental health problems often experience discrimination.	REALITY	Nine out of ten people with mental health problems experience stigma and discrimination.

Worksheet 1.2
Self-Harm Can Affect Anyone

Look at the images and read the quotations and descriptions. Try and match the correct description to the image of the person.

1 Pete Doherty   **A**   'I was hit with a massive wave of depression and anxiety and self-hatred, where the feelings were so painful I would slam my head against a tree to knock myself out. I never cut, but I'd scratch myself to the point of bleeding. I just wanted to dematerialise and have someone sweep me away.'

2 Sid Vicious   **B**   'It was a way of expressing my own shame, of myself, on my own body ... I was matching the inside to the outside. And there were some times where my emotions were just so built up, I didn't know what to do. The only way that I could get instant gratification was through an immediate release on myself.' They attended therapy and says that the support they received has changed their life.

3 Princess Diana   **C**   'My lowest point was Christmas Day 2008, because I didn't speak to my family ... I was struggling to deal with being alone and being forsaken and being betrayed by putting your trust in one person, and making the mistake of that being the wrong person. And that's a mistake that everyone can relate to. I made the mistake of trying to, desperately, grasp on and save that and own it. And every time I called her that day — I called 158 times — I took a razor blade and I cut myself on my face or on my hands.'

4 Marilyn Manson   **D**   'You have so much pain inside yourself that you try and hurt yourself on the outside because you want help, but it's the wrong help you're asking for. People see it as crying wolf or attention seeking ... I just hurt my arms and my legs; and I work in environments now where I see women doing similar things and I'm able to understand completely where they're coming from.'

5 Demi Lovato   **E**   Harmed themselves when performing on stage.

6 Cera Delevigne   **F**   Harmed themselves whilst being filmed for a BBC documentary in 2005. The BBC decided not to broadcast the footage.

Worksheet 1.3
Life Events that Lead Young People to Self-Harm

Schoolwork

Family death

Physical abuse

Parents fighting

Sexual abuse

Bullying

In trouble with the police

Friend's deliberate self-harm

Fights with friends

Fights with parents

Worksheet 1.4
Myths & Realities of Self-Harm

The Myth	The Reality
People who self-harm are attention seeking.	If attention was the reason for self-harming, there are far less painful and degrading ways of getting it. It is important to think of self-harm as attention *needing* rather than attention seeking.
People who self-harm are manipulative.	Self-harm is usually carried out in private. Much of the self-harming that occurs goes undiscovered. Many of those who self-harm go to great lengths to make sure it goes undiscovered.
Self-harmers need to see a psychiatrist in order to get better.	Psychiatry alone has had little success helping those who self-harm.
People who self-harm tend to be teenage girls and they grow out of it.	Recent research shows that there is less difference in the rates of self-injury between men and women than previously thought and there is no evidence that people 'grow out of it'.
People who talk about suicide do not mean to do it.	People who talk about suicide may be reaching out for help. Very many people contemplating suicide are experiencing anxiety, hopelessness and depression and may feel they have no other option. The experience of the *Samaritans* shows that many people who take their lives have given warning of their intentions in the weeks prior.
Self-harm is when you cut yourself.	There are many forms of self-harm, of which cutting is one. Others include scratching, self-hitting, self-poisoning, burning and head banging.
Young people self-harm to fit in with their peer group.	Self-harm is a response to emotional distress. Young people do not self-harm to fit in.
Self-harm is a rite of passage.	Self-harm is never just the usual part of adolescence. Young people self-harm if or when they experience real psychological pain and distress. It is not something that all young people do in response to such pain or stress as most will be able to use appropriate coping mechanisms and self-help strategies to manage these difficult times and emotions.
Taking about suicide encourages it.	Rather than encouraging the behaviour, talking openly about suicide can give the individual other options and time to rethink their decision.
If the injury isn't that bad – the problem can't be that bad.	Severity of emotional distress is not linked to the severity of the injury. It takes courage for someone to say that they have self-harmed and this must be taken seriously, regardless of how severe (or not) the injury is.

Reflections Worksheet 1
Identifying My Self-Harming Behaviours

We all do things that may not be good for us.

Try and list five things you do that may be harmful to yourself.

Give each one a rating of 0–5, depending on how harmful you think it may be, where 0 is not very harmful and 5 is most harmful.

What I do	Rating
1	0 1 2 3 4 5 Not harmful at all very harmful
2	0 1 2 3 4 5 Not harmful at all very harmful
3	0 1 2 3 4 5 Not harmful at all very harmful
4	0 1 2 3 4 5 Not harmful at all very harmful
5	0 1 2 3 4 5 Not harmful at all very harmful

Reflections Worksheet 1 — Identifying My Self-Harming Behaviours

List the things you do which you would like to change and those you would like to continue.

Give a reason for each one.

➤ **I would like to stop doing the following:**

Activity	Reason
Activity	Reason
Activity	Reason
Activity	Reason

➤ **I will carry on doing the following:**

Activity	Reason
Activity	Reason
Activity	Reason
Activity	Reason

Session 2
Understanding Stress & Anxiety

Introduction

In this session the group will be asked to consider the stresses that are placed upon them both at home and at school and to focus specifically upon how they do and can manage these stresses more effectively. As group members may identify personal experiences during this session, the activities need to be approached with sensitivity and care.

Give the group the opportunity to consider definitions for both stress and anxiety and how we can be affected both emotionally and physically in times of heightened stress. Explain that stresses can be specific to particular people (something that makes one person stressed may not stress someone else) and also that you will be talking about warning signs for possible anxiety disorders.

In the activities in this session, the group will learn about the importance of identifying how and when they feel stressed and of developing their own self-help strategies for when times get difficult or when stress levels increase. This is vital for young people in terms of preventing the escalation of problems and difficulties that could lead to the possible need to engage in self-harm in its various forms.

Defining stress is quite a difficult and complex process, given that it means different things to different people (in a similar vein to happiness, failure or success). Even though stress is a normal part of everyday life, too much stress can make young people become anxious, exhausted, tired and unable to function appropriately both inside and outside school. All of us have an optimum stress level that allows us to function effectively and efficiently in our daily lives - what is vital is that we learn how to recognise our own stress levels and develop coping strategies when we are experiencing higher than usual levels. This will enable us to maintain a healthy balance of tension, growth, rest and self-nurturing. We need to be able to focus and build up reactions that reduce stress, alongside understanding, acknowledging and coping effectively with the sources of our individual stresses.

Explain that young people who are experiencing higher levels of stress may exhibit the following behaviours:

- More aggressive or withdrawn behaviour
- Feeling tearful
- Eating disorders
- Self-harming behaviours
- School-attendance problems
- Need for attention
- Dropping performance
- Lying
- Heightened aggression

As well as the obvious stressors that occur in school, young people may face stressors outside school, for instance poverty, family disharmony, bereavement, abuse, and a change of home or school.

Anxiety is a normal response to a perceived threat and includes physical, emotional and mental responses, such as an increase in adrenalin, feelings of worry and confusion, and thoughts about danger and catastrophic outcomes. Normal levels of anxiety can help people to be more focused and motivated, and to solve problems more efficiently. However, chronic or high levels of anxiety can reduce a person's capacity to respond appropriately or effectively to stressful situations or even normal routine activities. For example, a highly anxious person may experience constant physical feelings of panic and may seek to avoid anything that might trigger their anxiety (such as being alone, going to school or talking in front of a group).

Anxiety may be triggered in many different ways. Sources of anxiety may include (but are not limited to) fear of:

- Social situations
- Negative evaluation and rejection
- Performing in public
- A specific object or situation (e.g., storms, lightning or thunder, insects, blood)
- Separation from a parent or carer
- A parent or carer being harmed
- Harm to oneself
- Academic performance and exams
- Starting school or work
- The future (what will happen, how it might turn out)

Anxiety may manifest as a number of physical symptoms, including muscle tension, shaking or trembling and heart palpitations, sweating or flushing, or feeling very hot or cold, amongst many others. In addition, children and young people experiencing anxiety may display a number of behavioural symptoms, including withdrawing from friends and family, avoidance of particular situations and negative thoughts or pessimism.

When the anxiety experienced by a young person starts to affect their general functioning, they may not just be feeling stressed – they may be suffering from an anxiety disorder. Anxiety disorders are considered serious mental health problems and are one of the most common mental health concerns for children and young people. Anxiety disorders are so common that one in four people will experience one or more anxiety disorders during their lifetime.

Icebreaker: How I Coped!

Ask the group to divide into smaller groups of four. Each small group should nominate a leader for discussions and also a scribe. Ask everyone to think about a stressful time in their lives and how they coped with it. Now explain that the discussion leaders should ask each person the following questions:

- What did help you when you were stressed?
- What didn't help you?

The scribes should record the responses from their group members about strategies that were and were not helpful.

Once everyone has finished, ask each small group to feedback to the larger group and record responses on a flipchart or whiteboard. Possible answers may include the following:

- Spending time with friends
- Taking exercise
- Playing on my computer
- 'Comfort' eating
- Having a drink
- Phoning a friend
- Talking to a close relative, for example, mum/dad, brother/sister
- Smoking
- Drinking
- Using social media
- Yoga
- Mindfulness

- Listening to music
- Watching a movie
- Doing something creative
- Relaxation techniques, for example, deep breathing

Look at and discuss the similarities and differences between people's responses as well as the merits and negative aspects of each strategy. For instance, alcohol and smoking may help you to feel more relaxed in the short term, but may lead to increased stress levels and poor sleeping patterns in the long term.

Note: It is important to emphasise that in this activity group members should not be asked to discuss their stressful experiences in any way that makes them feel uncomfortable or that may identify people who need to remain anonymous, but are allowed to share at their own comfort level. The important aspect of this activity is the coping strategies that people use.

Activities

2.1 The stressors in my life

Ask group members to think about the stressors they currently have in their lives and to consider what they can do in order to manage these more effectively. On Worksheet 2.1, 'The Stressors in My Life', each person can record three of these and then read through the different categories of stress-reducing strategies, adding some suggestions of their own to the existing lists. Finally, for each of the three stressors record possible strategies that could help to reduce or avoid this stress.

Reflections Worksheet

Give each person a copy of the Reflections Worksheet 2, 'Self-Help Strategies: "Five Looks" & Daily Stress Management Diary', which gives a summary of effective solution-focused stress management. Explain that this is an extremely useful strategy to develop and use. They can use this worksheet as a prompt sheet and on the second page of the worksheet is a 'Daily Stress Management Diary', which they can use every day to record the tools they use and how effective they find them.

These worksheets can be started in the session as a reinforcement activity and then carried on as a take-home task.

Discussion & Feedback

Ask the group to reflect on what they have learnt in the session, asking the following questions:

- What have we learnt in this session about the impact of stress on us as young people?
- What have we learnt about ways of managing stress?
- Do we all deal with stress in the same way?
- What new strategy or strategies might I try after today that I have not thought of before?

You can record the views, thoughts and feelings of the group members on a whiteboard or flipchart.

Worksheet 2.1
The Stressors in My Life

Try to think of three things that are currently causing stress in your life.

Look at the different categories of stress reducers; some ideas have already been completed. Try and add some more ideas of your own.

Now, for each of the things causing you stress, write one idea that you think could help to reduce or avoid this stress.

Three things that cause me stress are:

1	2	3

To reduce this stress I can:

1	2	3

Ideas for reducing stress

Show your feelings

- Cry.
- Talk to a friend.
- Write a poem.
- _____
- _____

Problem solve

- Write out the problem and brainstorm solutions.
- Work out strategies with a friend.
- Think about what is causing the stress and change what you are doing.
- _____
- _____

Find a distraction

- Learn a new skill.
- Try out a new computer game.
- Do something creative.
- _____
- _____

Nurture yourself

- Eat some chocolate.
- Have a bath.
- Watch your favourite television programme.
- _____
- _____

Problem solve

- Decide what is causing the stress and make a plan to tackle it.
- List as many solutions as possible. Try all the strategies until one works.
- _____
- _____
- _____

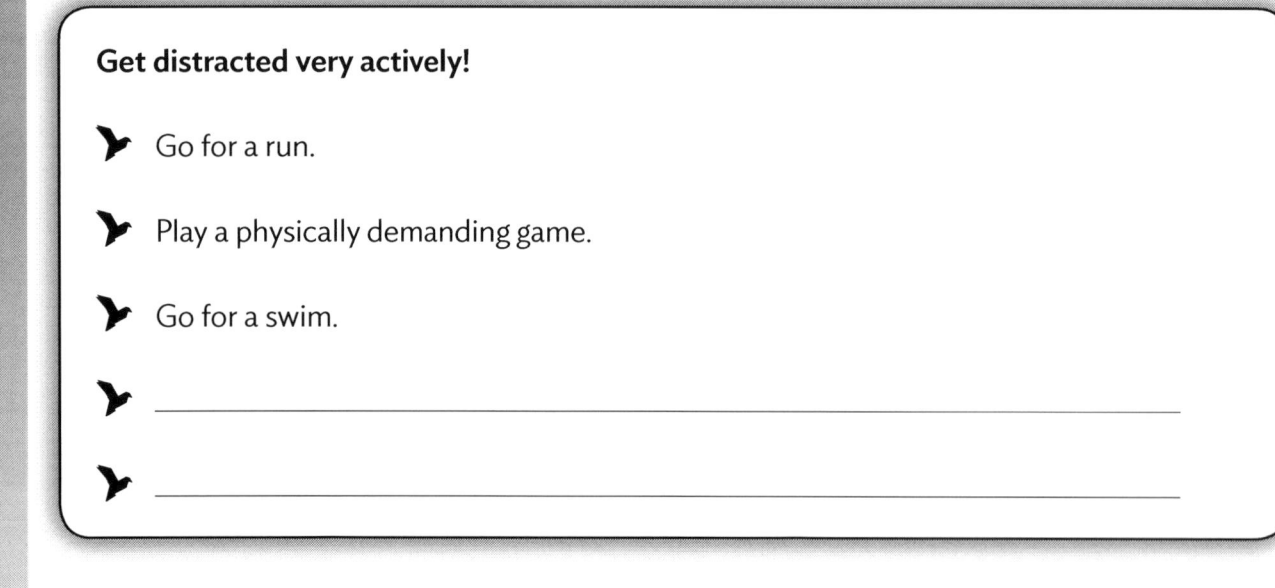

Get distracted very actively!

- Go for a run.
- Play a physically demanding game.
- Go for a swim.
- _____
- _____

Reflections Worksheet 2
Self-Help Strategies: 'Five Looks' & Daily Stress Management Diary

This worksheet describes a very useful strategy called 'Five Looks' that you can work on and use to help you to manage the stresses in your life.

Use this as a prompt sheet and try to keep an on-going diary of stress management to record on a daily basis which of the tools you use and how effective they have been.

Look about!

Try to measure the level of stress you are coping with.

Try to include usual daily hassles and things that you have adapted to recently. Remember – not all changes are negative BUT they may be a drain on your energy.

_____

_____

Look to yourself!

Try to regularly reflect on your own symptoms – are you getting anxious or irritable?

Are you trying to do too much or becoming inactive?

Try to identify any changes that may be due to a build-up of stress.

Try to THINK about the way you think, act and feel.

_____

_____

Page 1 of 3

Reflections Worksheet 2 Self-Help Strategies

Look forwards!

Always try to think about SOLUTIONS and particularly focus on whether the solutions you choose will be useful, both in the short and long term.

_____

_____

Look back!

Think about what worked before and learn from the most helpful and useful patterns of behaviour and strategies.

Try to learn from the less helpful responses – what could you do differently next time?

_____

_____

Look after yourself!

- Pace yourself and try to do one thing (for example, eat, rest, see friends, and so on) without doing other things at the same time.
- Use LISTS to aid memory and prioritise.
- Take breaks when the pressure builds up.
- Use breathing, relaxation and exercise and keep to a healthy diet and lifestyle.
- Give yourself treats and rewards.
- Try to reframe negative self-talk and respect yourself.
- Try to enjoy life and your relationships!

Daily Stress Management Diary

Every day write down something that caused you stress and what you did.

Then rate the effectiveness of your strategy from 0 to 10, where 0 is ineffective and 10 is very effective.

In the last column think if you would do anything next time to help you even more.

Use the 'Five Looks' to remind yourself of different ideas.

Day	Stress	What I did	How effective was it?	What would I do differently next time to cope more effectively?
			0 1 2 3 4 5 6 7 8 9 10 *Not effective at all ↔ very effective*	
			0 1 2 3 4 5 6 7 8 9 10 *Not effective at all ↔ very effective*	
			0 1 2 3 4 5 6 7 8 9 10 *Not effective at all ↔ very effective*	
			0 1 2 3 4 5 6 7 8 9 10 *Not effective at all ↔ very effective*	
			0 1 2 3 4 5 6 7 8 9 10 *Not effective at all ↔ very effective*	
			0 1 2 3 4 5 6 7 8 9 10 *Not effective at all ↔ very effective*	
			0 1 2 3 4 5 6 7 8 9 10 *Not effective at all ↔ very effective*	

Reflections Worksheet 2 Self-Help Strategies

Session 3

Triggers & Traumas: The Impact of Social Media & the Internet

Introduction

This session looks at actions and activities that may be engaged in by young people when they access social media sites. The aim is to highlight some of the pressures that may be experienced by young people when they see images of perfection and excellence and to consider the emotional, physical and social impacts of these. There is a particular focus on the use of self-harm websites and opportunities for discussion as to whether these are useful or whether they can act as triggers to young people. The group will be asked to engage in a debate as to whether or not they think these should be banned or simply policed more effectively.

Icebreaker: Body Images in the Media

Prior to this activity you will need to collect a number of images of both men and women from magazines, the internet, and so on. Try to find a mix of well-known people and advertisements showing people of different ages, shapes and sizes and different images of the same people. Explain that in this activity the group will be asked to consider a range of images taken from the media. In small groups of four, ask the students to:

- Note down some words that come to mind when they see these images (e.g., wife, father, age, aging, ethnicity, weight, masculinity sexualised).

- Think about and identify where the sexualisation of women and men occurs and provide examples – music videos, TV, films, magazines, newspapers (think about the 'No more page 3' campaign, or the campaign against the 'Are You Beach Body Ready?' advertisement), coverage of sporting events ('This Girl Can' – women in sport campaign), video games.

- Consider whether any of these images have been airbrushed or photo-shopped?

- Now think about whether the same pressures around body image are felt by boys and men. Have these pressures increased recently?

- Finally, consider these facts and discuss what the implications might be for the well-being of girls and boys, and young men and young women:
  - We see these images more than we see our own family members.
  - The current media ideal of thinness for women is achievable by less than 5 percent of the female population.
  - Fifty per cent of the images of women we see in the media portray women with a BMI that is unhealthy (i.e., not enough body fat).

Activities

3.1 Self-harm websites: the debate

Explain to the group that you will be looking at issues around self-harm and the internet, and that they are going to be holding a debate about whether self-harm websites should be regulated.

Using Worksheet 3.1, 'Self-Harm Websites: The Debate', begin by introducing the group to the findings from the NSPCC's 2015 report examining the reasons why children contacted *ChildLine*.

- 700 children and young people aged between 12 and 13 years old were surveyed.
- 1 in 10 were worried they are addicted to porn.
- More than 1 in 10 had themselves made, or had been part of, a sexually explicit video.
- Peter Liver (Director of *ChildLine* in 2015) has reported that children said watching porn made them feel depressed, gave them body image problems and that they felt pressured to engage in sexual acts they were not ready for.
- A report from the charity CHILDWISE (92013/4) revealed that the website 'Pornhub' was among the top five favourite sites for boys aged 11 to 16.

Discuss whether any of these findings are surprising to the group.

Lead the discussion on to information relating specifically to self-harm websites and the impact of these on young people. Share copies of the summary of the *Young Minds* article (Worksheet 3.1) to discuss in pairs, before feeding back to the whole group.

- One in five school children with a history of self-harm and eating disorders questioned by researchers at Oxford and Stirling Universities said *they first learnt about these after seeing or reading something online,* second only to hearing about it from friends.
- The Royal College of Psychiatrists says it is now 'seriously concerned' about the growing number of websites that glamorise the problem of self-harm or show gory images of cuts and scars.

Now divide the group into two smaller groups and introduce the debate. This will involve a particular focus on the use of self-harm websites and a discussion as to whether these are useful or simply triggering to young people. The title of the debate is:

Should self-harm websites be banned or simply policed more effectively?

In order to give some further background for the debate, give the group the following link to an article in *The Guardian,* which details some of the concerns young people have about their friends' self-harming behaviours.

http://www.theguardian.com/society/2014/mar/10/self-harm-sites-cyberbullying-suicide-web

One of the sub-groups will argue that self-harm websites should be banned and the other group will argue that they need to be policed more effectively, rather than banned completely. Decide whether you will act as the judge in the debate or whether the whole group should vote on the winning argument at the end of the debate. Ensure before you start everyone is clear about how the debate will be decided.

Explain that each group will have 15 minutes to prepare their ideas, after which they will each have 10 minutes to present their argument to the whole group. Using the prompt sheets in Worksheet 3.1, they should aim to come up with three main arguments or more if they wish.

Each group can either choose a 'speaker' to present their side of the debate, or the task could be shared between all group members.

Once each group has made their main presentation, they can each have a further 5 minutes to make any finals arguments or challenge what the other side has said.

Finally, lead a discussion with the whole group to summarise the ideas they have raised. If the whole group are going to vote on the winning argument this should be done now. If there is a tie, you can provide the deciding vote. If you alone are to choose the winning side, ensure that you explain your reasons clearly.

Reflections Worksheet

Ask the group to think about their relationship with the internet and social media – the positives and the negatives and what they can do to keep healthy and safe.

Give everyone a copy of Reflections Worksheet 3, 'My Relationship with the Internet', and then talk through the different sections using the examples below. Group members may find it helpful to work in pairs or small groups when completing the final two boxes of the worksheet.

Points for discussion

The internet is not a simple force for good or bad in the lives of young people – like most things, the internet is user-sensitive. This Reflections Worksheet 3 will help students to think about their own relationship with the internet and social media.

Internet usage becomes an ingrained habit and many people visit the same relatively small collection of websites day after day. As a result, thinking about their current habits invites the group to think about more positive habits they could acquire.

Positives about the internet – what do the group see as the ways in which the internet is a helpful and useful aspect of their day-to-day lives? For example:

- Helping with school work
- Keeping in touch with friends and family

Negatives about the internet – what do the group perceive as the negatives? For example:

- Pressure to look a certain way (from adverts or social media)
- Feeling left out socially
- Staying up late online and then being tired
- Spending too long online (e.g., playing games or looking at videos and then not doing things they want or need to do, such as playing sport or doing homework).

Healthy inter\net habits – what ideas can the group think of which could help to combat these negatives, for example:

- Don't use any dangerous or unsafe websites (delete them from favourites and browsing history).
- Have set hours for not going online (e.g., not after 10pm on week nights).
- Bear in mind at all times that images we see online and in the media are airbrushed, digitally edited and unrealistic.
- Use a timer or alarm to control internet and computer usage.
- Deactivate online accounts (e.g., Facebook and Twitter) for a few days.

Distractions to avoid unhealthy internet habits – as well as finding healthy ways of using the internet (see above). Ask the group to think of some fun distractions:

- Turn off the smart phone or computer and go into another room.
- Go for a run or go to the gym.
- Go and talk to someone.
- Draw, colour in a pattern, or write in a journal.
- Instead of sending an email, a text or a tweet – write a letter or postcard to a friend.
- Take the dog for a walk.

Discussion & Feedback

Ask the group to reflect on what they have learnt in the session, asking the following question:

What have we learned about helpful and unhelpful ways of using the internet?

Record the responses in two columns on a whiteboard or flipchart and emphasise the helpful and safe factors for young people to consider when using the internet.

Worksheet 3.1
Self-Harm Websites: The Debate

NSPCC'S 2015 SURVEY

- 700 young people surveyed aged 12 and 13.
- 1 in 10 were worried they were addicted to porn.
- More than 1 in 10 had made/been part of sexually explicit video.
- Peter Liver (Director of Child Line) reports that children have said watching porn makes them feel depressed, gives them body image problems and they feel pressured to engage in sexual acts they are not ready for.
- A report from the charity Childwise (92013/4) – revealed the website Pornhub was among the top 5 favourite sites for boys aged 11 from 16.

Information about self-harm from *YoungMinds'* website

Online Impact

- One in five school children with a history of self-harm and eating disorders questioned by researchers at Oxford and Stirling Universities said *they first learnt about it after seeing or reading something online,* second only to hearing about it from friends.

- The Royal College of Psychiatrists says it is now 'seriously concerned' about the growing number of websites that glamorise the problem or show gory images of cuts and scars.

Prompt Sheet: Self-Harm Websites Should be Banned

Your group will be presenting arguments as to why self-harm websites should be banned.

In your group, discuss these ideas and questions. One person in the group should record your thoughts, so they can form your main arguments for the debate:

- What impact do self-harm websites have?
- Who do they affect?
- What would you hope would happen if self-harm websites were banned?
- Why is banning outright better than 'policing more effectively'?

Our group's three main arguments:

(You can have more!)

⭐ 1 _____

⭐ 2 _____

⭐ 3 _____

Page 2 of 3

Prompt Sheet: Self-Harm Websites should be Policed more Effectively, not Banned Completely

Your group will be presenting arguments as to why self-harm websites should not be banned completely, but should instead be policed more effectively.

In your group, discuss these ideas and questions. One person in the group should record your thoughts, so they can form your main arguments for the debate:

- What impact do self-harm websites have?
- Who do they affect?
- What would you hope for if self-harm websites were more effectively policed?
- Why is 'policing more effectively' a better choice than banning self-harm websites?
- How could self-harm websites be 'policed more effectively'?

Our group's three main arguments:

(You can have more!)

1 _____

2 _____

3 _____

Reflections Worksheet 3
My Relationship with the Internet

Ways in which the internet helps me:

➤ _____

➤ _____

➤ _____

Negatives about the internet:

➤ _____

➤ _____

➤ _____

Healthy internet habits:

➤ _____

➤ _____

➤ _____

My distractions:

➤ _____

➤ _____

➤ _____

Session 4

Preventing Self-Harm & Reducing Risk: Key Tools & Strategies

Introduction

This session focuses on the supporting group to identify the strategies they have already developed to cope with stress and to further to develop new skills to support their positive mental health and well-being. In this session, the group members will be asked to remember and reflect on how they have coped in the past at stressful or difficult times in their lives. Consequently you will need to ensure that any discussions are treated sensitively.

Icebreaker: Alternatives to Self-Harming

Discuss with the group the following list of alternatives to self-harming in times of stress and ask which they think people who feel like self-harming might find most useful and why. While some of these alternatives might seem unusual, many of them have been recommended by young people as effective distractors from self-harm. The group could also consider if any of these strategies might trigger others around them to feel stressed or even prompt self-harming or copy-cat behaviours if used in the school context.

Alternatives for when you're feeling angry or restless:

- Scribble on photos of people in magazines.
- Viciously stab an orange.
- Throw an apple or pair of socks against the wall.
- Have a pillow fight with a wall.
- Scream very loudly.
- Tear apart newspapers, photos or magazines.
- Go to the gym, dance or exercise.

- Listen to music and sing along loudly.
- Draw a picture of what is making you angry.
- Beat up a stuffed bear.
- Pop bubble wrap.
- Pop balloons.
- Splatter paint.
- Scribble on a piece of paper until the whole page is black.
- Fill a piece of paper by drawing cross hatches.
- Throw darts at a dartboard.
- Go for a run.
- Write your feelings on paper then rip it up.
- Use stress relievers.
- Build a fort of pillows and then destroy it.
- Throw ice cubes at the bath tub, a wall, at a tree.
- Slash an empty plastic bottle, or a piece of heavy cardboard, or an old shirt or sock.
- Make a soft cloth doll to represent the things you are angry at; cut and tear it instead of yourself.
- Flatten aluminium cans for recycling, seeing how fast you can go.
- On a sketch or photo of yourself, mark in red ink what you want to do. Cut and tear the picture.
- Break sticks.
- Cut up fruit.
- Make yourself as comfortable as possible.
- Stomp around in heavy shoes.
- Play handball or tennis.
- Buy a cheap plate and decorate it with markers, stickers, cut-outs from magazines, words, images – whatever expresses your pain or sadness. When you've finished, smash it. (Although be careful when doing this!).
- Use a 'Calm Jar' as follows: fill a jar with coloured water and glitter. When feeling upset or angry you can shake it to disturb the glitter and focus on that until the glitter settles.
- Blow up a balloon and pop it.
- Yell at anything you are breaking or tearing up and tell it why you are angry, or hurt, or upset, and so on.

Alternatives that will give you a sensation (other than pain) without harming yourself:

- Hold ice in your hands, against your arm, or in your mouth.
- Run your hands under freezing cold water.
- Snap a rubber band or hair band against your wrist.
- Clap your hands until they sting.
- Wax your legs.
- Drink freezing cold water.
- Splash your face with cold water.
- Put PVA glue on your hands then peel it off.
- Massage where you want to hurt yourself.
- Take a hot shower/bath.
- Jump up and down to get some sensation in your feet.
- Write or paint on yourself.
- Arm wrestle with a member of your family.
- Take a cold bath.
- Bite into a hot pepper or chew a piece of ginger root.
- Rub liniment under your nose.

Activities

4.1 Work on things step-by-step: developing a personal prevention or safety plan

In this activity, the group are asked to consider what they would include in a personal self-harm prevention or safety plan. A prevention or safety plan can be created by a young person to give them an actual document they can use to help them think through different possible strategies to support them when they are feeling overwhelmed or upset. It is important to ensure that you allow enough time for each young person to think through the different stages and questions when completing their own crisis plan.

This activity is intended to support the development of coping mechanisms and a reduction of self-harm in those already engaged in such behaviours. It is vital that they see that they can begin to take more control and plan for their own well-being and safety more effectively. It can, however, also be used as a means of planning for stressful events for those who may not be engaging in self-harm at present, but may well have thought about going down this route when very stressed and unable to effectively engage with support mechanisms or coping strategies.

NOTE: Group members will be asked to review these safety plans in Session 8, so they will need to bring them back in for this session.

Give each group member a copy of Worksheet 4.1, 'My Personal Self-Harm Prevention or Safety Plan'. Then introduce the following questions as prompts for thought. Ask everybody to compete the worksheet in as much detail as they find helpful.

- What have you found helpful at stressful times in the past? Jot these things down and make sure you include them on your plan.
- Think about whether you want as many options as possible on the plan, or would a very long list be too overwhelming?
- Do you find it hard to make decisions in a crisis? If so, you might find it helpful to number the list in a fixed order that you'll work through, or make it a flow chart.
- How would you like to decorate your list? You could include colours and pictures that you find soothing, uplifting or even funny.

A safety plan is something that reminds you what you can do and where you can turn when you feel overwhelmed. It can be very helpful if you are feeling unable to cope or if you feel like you might hurt yourself.

Some young people may find it helpful to keep a detailed safety plan in their bedroom and then a brief version on a card in their wallet or purse. Suggest that group members could design their own, wallet-sized version once they have completed their safety plans.

Reflections Worksheet

Introduce the group to the idea of mindfulness and how taking time for some mindful moments can help to reduce stresses and anxiety. Give each person a copy of Reflections Worksheet 4, 'Getting the Mindfulness Habit'.

Mindfulness can be thought of as the ability to remain aware of how you are feeling at that moment. Thinking about the past, blaming or judging yourself, or worrying about the future can often lead to a degree of stress that is overwhelming. However, by staying calm and paying more attention in the present moment, you can bring yourself 'back into balance', which can improve mental well-being.

'Mindfulness meditations' can help by bringing you into the present while you focus your attention on a single repetitive action, such as your breathing, a few repeated words, or flickering light from a candle.

Evidence shows that what we do and the way we think about things have the biggest impact on well-being.

Key points in mindfulness mediation are:

- A quiet space, where you can relax without distractions or being interrupted.
- Get comfortable, but avoid lying down as this may lead to you falling asleep! You may meditate with eyes open or closed.
- A point of focus, such as your breathing, a few repeated words, or flickering light from a candle.
- Don't worry about distracting thoughts that go through your mind or about how well you're doing. If thoughts intrude during your relaxation session, don't fight them. Instead, gently turn your attention back to your point of focus.

Explain that mindfulness meditation can take some time to be able to do effectively, and that the group should use the worksheet to practise at home.

Discussion & Feedback

Ask the group to reflect on what they have learnt during the session, some key points to include are as follows:

- Why is it important that we know our own emotional 'triggers' which upset us?
- How has this session helped us to think about the relationship between thoughts and habits?
- Distractions are in important strategy to help us to break unhelpful routines and habits – what new distractions will you think about trying?

Worksheet 4.1
My Personal Self-Harm Prevention or Safety Plan

Before you start to complete your plan, read through and think about the following ideas and steps to building your plan.

If self-harming has already become a kind of coping strategy for you, it is not usually helpful to focus on complete abstinence or banning the behaviour in one sudden step. Instead, it is helpful to build new strategies for dealing with difficult feelings: these can gradually take the place of self-harm. In the first instance it can be useful to consider learning first aid and knowing how to take care of yourself practically if you do self-harm.

Creating a personal self-harm safety plan is a useful way to remind yourself of things you can do when you feel an urge to self-harm. These include ways to manage and reduce self-harming behaviours in the short term, so that they are less damaging, as well as finding alternative ways to manage difficult feelings that can replace self-harm in the longer term.

Even if you have not previously self-harmed, this prevention or safety plan can also be used as a helpful tool for those times when you feel very stressed and not able to effectively engage your support mechanisms or coping strategies.

De-escalate the intensity of self-harm

A first step can be to think about trying to slowly reduce the damage caused by your self-harming behaviour (e.g., cutting less deeply). Then try to move to less damaging practices, such as writing on your skin with red felt-tip instead of cutting.

Direct the harming urge at something else

Some people find squeezing an ice cube provides an alternative that is helpful. Hit pillows or cushions. Flick an elastic band on your wrist. Take a cold bath or shower.

Make a list of activities that you can use to distract yourself

Trying to be with other people is particularly effective.

Know your triggers and reduce the risks

Knowing what kinds of situations are particularly risky for you can help you plan to reduce the risks. For example, it is harder to manage your feelings effectively when you are under the influence of drugs or alcohol. Go easy on these if you are aware that you are feeling less stable.

Learn to tune in to your feelings

In the longer-term you can start to learn how to identify the experiences and feelings that are most likely to trigger your urges to self-harm. Learning the skill of 'mindfulness' – being tuned in to what you are feeling in the present moment, without judgement or attempt to change it – is invaluable in the move towards being able to manage or 'ride out' difficult feelings, rather than trying to eliminate them.

My Personal Self-Harm Prevention or Safety Plan

What makes me want to harm myself? For example, it could be particular people, feelings, places or memories.

Other than harming myself, what else helps me to cope?

What would I tell a close friend to do who was feeling this way?

What could others do that would help?

```
┌─────────────────────────────────────────────────────────────────┐
│                                                                 │
│                                                                 │
│                                                                 │
│                                                                 │
└─────────────────────────────────────────────────────────────────┘
```

If I feel like harming myself again, I will do one of the following (try to list 6-8 items):

1. _____
2. _____
3. _____
4. _____
5. _____
6. _____
7. _____
8. _____

If the plan does not work and I still feel like harming myself, I will do at least one of the following:

- ➤ Call the *Samaritans* on **116 123** (free calls)
- ➤ Call *ChildLine* on **0800 1111** (free calls)
- ➤ Talk to a trusted adult _____
- ➤ Call emergency services **999** or go to nearest A&E

Signed: _____ Date: _____

Worksheet 4.1 My Personal Self-Harm Prevention or Safety Plan

Reflections Worksheet 4
Getting the Mindfulness Habit

Mindfulness is a way of paying attention to the present moment. When we're mindful we become more aware of our thoughts and feelings and better able to manage them.

Being mindful can boost our concentration, improve our relationships and help with stress or depression. It can even have a positive effect on physical problems like chronic pain.

Anyone can learn to be mindful. It's simple, you can do it anywhere, and the results can be life-changing.

Take 10 minutes each day to do a simple mindfulness meditation

Many of us spend much of our time focused either on the past or on the future, paying very little attention to what is happening right now.

Being mindful involves staying in the moment, spending more time noticing what's going on, both inside ourselves and in our surroundings. Rather than trying to change things, it involves accepting the way that things are, for better or for worse.

You can follow a free 10-day daily guided meditations on the Headspace website:

www.getsomeheadspace.com

Session 5

Supporting Friends who Self-Harm: Key Issues & Sources of Support

Introduction

This session focuses on building the group's understanding of self-harm and introducing possible strategies for them to think about in order to try to help people they believe may be self-harming. It is important during this session that you are not seen as judgemental by condemning self-harm or giving the impression of encouraging it as a coping strategy; rather, the focus is on encouraging alternatives to self-harm.

Icebreaker: People Who Help Me

For this activity ask the group to sit in a large circle around the room. Using the circle-time tool of 'rounds', begin the icebreaker by completing the following sentences yourself:

- Somebody who helps me when I have a problem is …
- They help me by …

Then each person takes a turn around the circle to complete the same sentences.

You could conclude by summarising the sorts of people who the group find supportive, for example, friends, family members, teachers, as well as the type of support that they find helpful.

Now ask the group to consider the question: How would I cope if my friend told me he or she was self-harming due to not being able to cope with the stress in their lives?

Understanding & Preventing Self-Harm in Schools

It may be helpful for you to list on the board the ideas and contributions that group members make and to highlight those that may be the most helpful. What is essential here is to reinforce the need for responding with kindness and care and not to reject or seem to be angry or disgusted in any way by their friends' revelations.

Activities

5.1 Supporting friends who are under stress

For this activity ask the group to complete Worksheet 5.1, 'Supporting Friends who are Under Stress'. They will need to think of ways they might be able to spot if a friend is stressed or self-harming and then to think of things they might do in response, which could be either helpful or unhelpful.

5.2 Helping friends who self-harm

Before the session make copies of Worksheet 5.2, 'Helping Friends who Self-Harm', and cut out the cards into sets. Divide everyone into smaller groups of about three or four people and give each group a set of the cards. Explain that these contain suggestions of how we might help friends who self-harm.

Each group should discuss the cards and try to decide how effective they believe each suggestion to be and then place the cards into two piles, one for helpful suggestions and one for unhelpful.

Once the small groups have done this, discuss in the whole group the decisions made about the suggestions and write these on the board along with the reasons for choices.

The suggested responses are as follows:

Helpful	Unhelpful
Talk to them about it.	Tell them to stop it. (If they could they would already have done so.)
Tell a responsible adult.	Tell their other friends so you can all help together. (They have chosen to talk to you, not necessarily their other friends. You should not break this trust.)
Listen to them.	Talk to their parents about it (although you could encourage them to do this, it would not be a good idea to do this behind their back. They may then stop talking about it altogether.)
Find out information for them.	Ask to see their injuries. (Those who self-harm often experience feelings of shame afterwards; asking to see their injuries will only add to this. You can encourage them to seek medical help if they think their injuries need attention.)
Encourage them to get professional help.	Tell them to wear long sleeves to keep their injuries covered up. (Again this may add to the person's sense of shame about their actions. If the person is allowing their injuries to be seen it may also mean they are at a stage where they are ready to receive help.)
Offer to go with them to see a counsellor.	Tell them you won't talk to them unless they stop. (This will leave the young person feling even worse and alone.)

Reflections Worksheet

Give each person a copy of Reflections Worksheet 5, 'My Safety Net'. Discuss how we all have different people in different types of groups in our lives, for instance, family, friends, regular acquaintances, and professionals we meet regularly. These groups can be in our immediate circle or at more distance from us.

Ask everyone to try to think of some people from each of these groups who they might feel safe and comfortable talking to and to write their names on the worksheet:

- Family and close friends
- Friends and people I see very regularly or every day
- Professional people (in or out of school), or helplines I could go to for support

Group members can use the worksheet as a reminder of people who could be helpful at times of stress and anxiety.

Discussion & Feedback

The main purpose of this session is to increase the group's understanding of self-harm and to give them possible strategies for helping people they believe may be self-harming. It is vital that the facilitator does not condemn self-harm, but must also not be seen to encourage it as a coping strategy, rather to offer alternatives to self-injury.

The facilitator may conclude by summarising the people who are supportive for the group (for example, friends, family, teachers, and so on), the kind of support students find helpful, while highlighting relevant and useful sources of support for the students.

Ask the group to reflect on what they have learnt in the session, focusing on the following questions:

- What have we learned about self-harm?
- What do we consider the best way to help friends who self-harm?
- Where can we get help and support?
- What should we not do if our friend confides in us?

You could record the students' responses on a whiteboard or flipchart.

Worksheet 5.1
Supporting Friends who are Under Stress

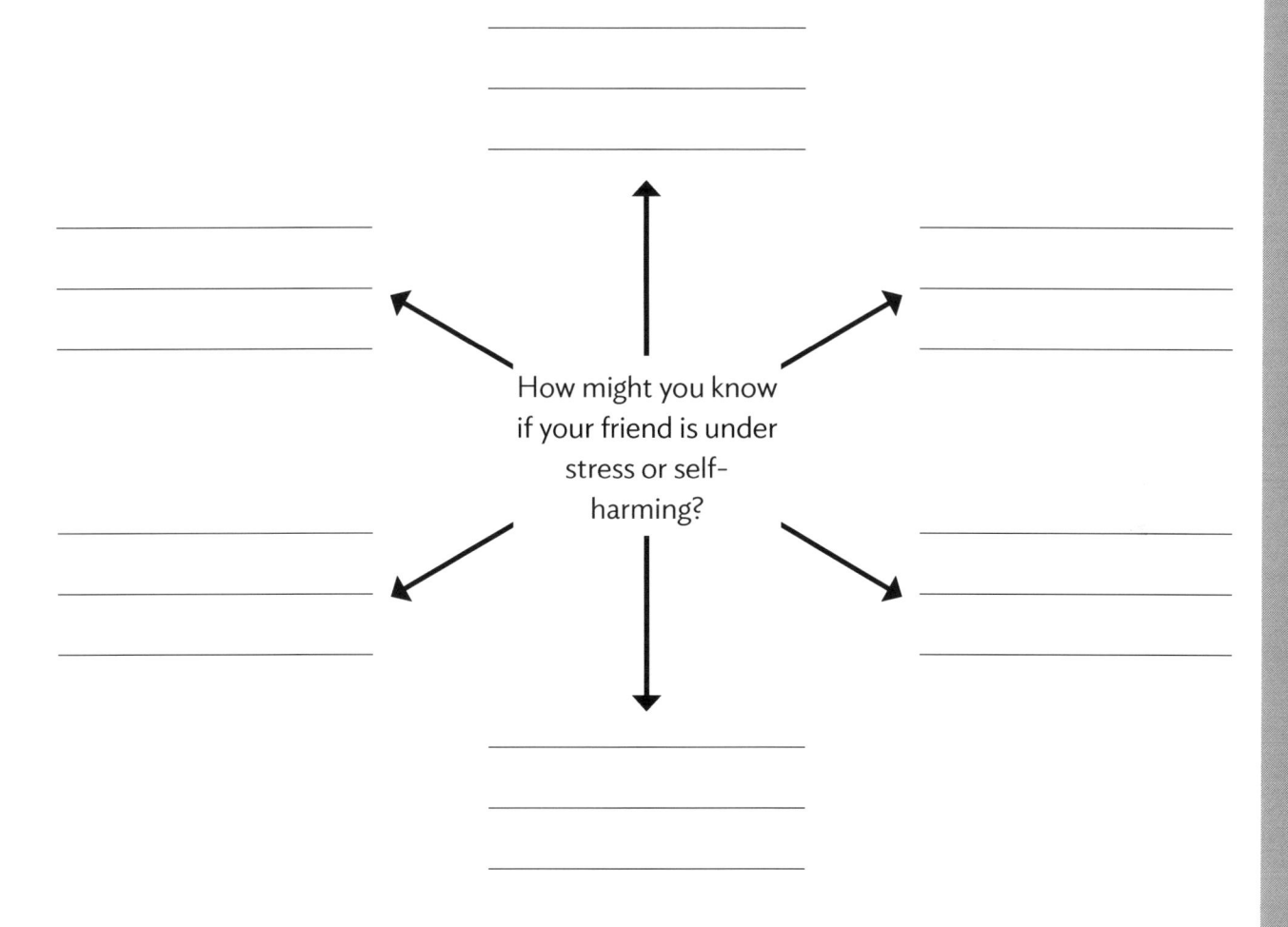

How might you know if your friend is under stress or self-harming?

List as many things as you can think of that may, and may not, be helpful.

Helpful	Unhelpful

Worksheet 5.2
Helping Friends who Self-Harm

Make copies of this worksheet and cut out the cards before the session starts. Give each smaller group a set of cards.

Discuss each option within groups and then divide the suggestions into two piles of 'helpful' and 'unhelpful'.

Why did you make these choices?

Tell them to 'stop it'.

Talk to them about it.

Tell a responsible adult.

Listen to them.

Find out information for them.

Encourage them to get professional help.

Offer to go with them to see a counsellor.

Tell their other friends so you can all help together.

Talk to their parents about it.

Ask to see their injuries.

Tell them to make sure they wear long sleeves to keep their cuts covered up.

Reflections Worksheet 5
My Safety Net

We all have different people in different types of groups in our lives, for instance, family, friends, regular acquaintances, and professionals we meet regularly. These groups can be in our immediate circle or more distant from us.

Try to think about people in each of these groups who you would feel safe and comfortable talking to, and write their names on the diagram, starting from your immediate circle of family and close friends.

- Family and close friends.
- Friends and people I see very regularly or every day.
- Professional people (in or out of school), or helplines I could go to for support.

Once you have added the people you trust you could also add thoughts, activities or places that could be part of your safety net and help to support you.

If you are feeling creative why not draw your own safety net? It can be any shape you like, for example, the leaves on a tree or a hand.

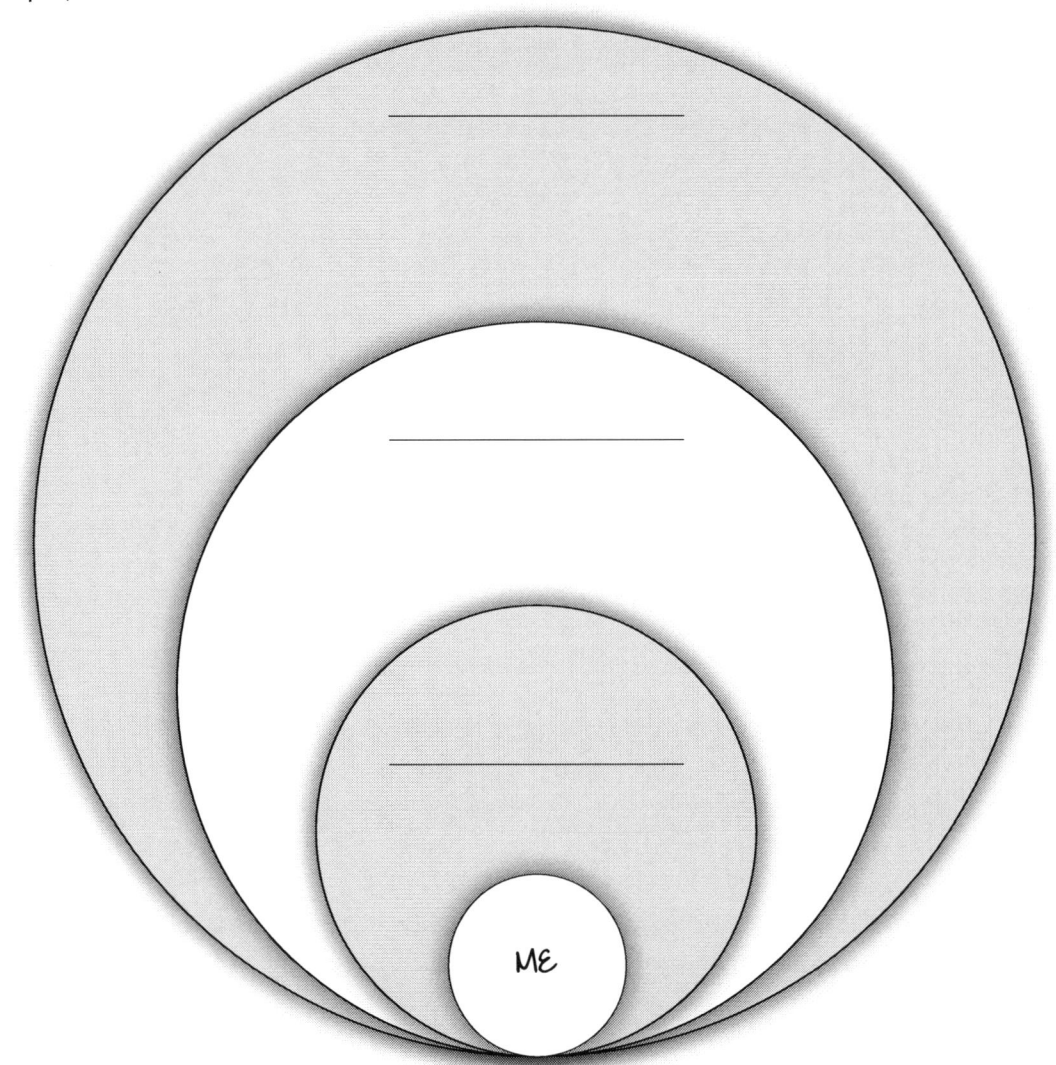

ME

Session 6

Key Tools from Cognitive Behavioural Therapy (CBT) to Practise and Use

Introduction

Cognitive behavioural therapy (CBT) focuses on the role that thoughts play with regard to both emotions and behaviour, and advocates that changes in thought processes can have a significant effect upon altering behaviours. Unlike many of the talking treatments that therapists have traditionally used, CBT focuses upon the 'here and now', as well as ways to improve the individual state of mind in the present time. This is innovative in the sense that there is no focus on the causes of distress or on past symptoms as there is with traditional psychotherapy.

Restructuring thought processes

Young people are frequently flooded with anxious and negative thoughts and doubts. These messages will often reinforce a state of inadequacy and/or low levels of **self-esteem**. The process of CBT helps to support young people in reconsidering these negative assumptions. It also allows them to *learn how* to change their self-perceptions, in order to improve their mental and emotional state – this is the key aim of this type of intervention. Changing negative thought patterns or opinions will ultimately help young people to become more able to control and change their behaviours, but this does take practice. This is why, as with anger management interventions, another key element of the approach is the requirement to learn, and to put into practice, the skills or strategies required.

ABC

The CBT approach breaks a particular problem into three smaller parts:

- **A:** the **activating event** is often referred to as the 'trigger' – the thing that causes someone to engage in negative thinking.
- **B:** represents these negative **beliefs**, which can include thoughts, rules and demands, and the meanings the individual attaches to both external and internal events.

- **C: the consequences**, or emotions, and the behaviours and physical sensations accompanying these different emotions. It is important to highlight and discuss with the group the idea that the way in which they think about a problem can affect how they feel physically and emotionally. It can also alter what they do about it. This is why the key aim for CBT is to break the negative, vicious cycle that some young people may find themselves in. For example, if you think that you will get your work wrong you feel angry, and then you do not give it a try in case you get it wrong.

Core Beliefs

Core beliefs are the strong, enduring ideas that we may have about ourselves. This kind of belief system gives rise to rules, demands or assumptions, which in turn produce automatic thoughts. Core beliefs generally fall into three main categories: beliefs about yourself; beliefs about other people in the world; beliefs that are either positive or negative. What is important is to identify our core beliefs and to also consider why these may or may not be unhelpful. In this way we can begin to identify 'Negative Automatic Thoughts' (NATs). Some of these negative thoughts that young people may hold about themselves could include the following:

- I always look ugly.
- I don't understand this work.
- He thinks I'm stupid and an idiot.
- She gave me a nasty look.
- I'm just such a useless person.
- I can't do that and I'll never be able to do it like other people can.

When working with young people in identifying such faulty thinking, the main aim is to encourage them to break the negative cycle. These NATs can arise from a number of errors in our thinking, including the following six types of faulty thinking:

- Doing ourselves down – only focusing on the negatives and seeing bad things about ourselves.
- Blowing things up or catastrophising – making things worse than they really are.
- Predicting failure – setting your mind ready to predict failure at all costs.
- Over-emotional thoughts – this is when your emotions become extremely powerful and cloud your judgment.
- Setting yourself up – setting yourself targets that are too high so that you know then you will fail.
- Blaming yourself – thinking that everything that goes wrong is your own fault.

When working with young people, it is important to allow them time to consider the effects that these NATs can have, prior to them beginning to implement some changes.

This session will introduce the group to some of these thinking errors, whilst also encouraging them to make use, on a more regular basis, of more effective thinking as well as learning to reframe the negative automatic thoughts that they have. This is essential in terms of preventing the escalation of difficulties and stressors.

Ultimately, if we are able to use these tools, then we should be able to decrease the level of automatic thinking that we engage in. This is particularly important for young people when they are forming their sense of self and beginning to experience a wider range of stressors as they enter into adolescence. If they have a range of tools to reduce NATs and increase coping mechanisms and positive thinking then they are also less likely to fall into the trap or habit of self-harming behaviours.

Icebreaker: Introducing CBT

Give each member of the group copies of the CBT information sheets (Worksheet 6.1, 'Using Cognitive Behavioural Therapy (CBT) Skills'). Explain that the key concept of CBT is understanding the links between our thoughts, feelings and behaviours. How we think about something affects how we feel about it and also how we behave. Look at the examples of some of these links on the worksheet and discuss these in the group.

Explain that these are examples of core beliefs that come from NATs (negative automatic thoughts) and that these arise from errors in the way we think. Core beliefs very often are formulated in early childhood and are the result of the messages we may have been given by parents/carers and others in our social environment. Sometimes these are helpful to us and sometimes they can become unhelpful, for example, my core belief may be that it is important to be a good and kind person, but this may not be helpful if my kindness is met with abuse and bullying: I then think it is all my fault and that I am not such a good or kind person. Examples of thinking errors are:

- Doing ourselves down – only focusing on the negatives and seeing bad things about ourselves.
- Blowing things up or catastrophising – making things worse than they really are.
- Predicting failure – setting your mind ready to predict failure at all costs.
- Over-emotional thoughts – this is when your emotions become extremely powerful and cloud your judgment.
- Setting yourself up – setting yourself targets that are too high so that you know then you will fail.
- Blaming yourself – thinking that everything that goes wrong is your own fault.

These thinking errors, or NATs, can lead to anxiety and low self-esteem.

Activities

6.1 Test the evidence

One of the most helpful interventions for developing new and more positive belief systems, and for challenging these negative automatic thoughts, is to test the evidence. When introducing this activity, outline the kind of negative thoughts group members might want to choose to challenge – you can go back to the previous examples from the start of the session to use as prompts.

Using Worksheet 6.2, 'Testing the Evidence', ask the group members to come up with one of their core beliefs and to follow the questioning process in order to test the evidence for their belief:

1. What is the evidence for this thought?
2. What is the evidence against this thought?
3. What would my best friend say if they heard my thought?
4. What would my teacher say if they heard my thought?
5. What would my parents or carers say if they heard my thought?
6. What would I say to my best friend if they had this same thought?
7. Am I making mistakes? For example, blowing it up, forgetting my strengths or good points, self-blaming or predicting failure, or thinking that I can mind-read what others are thinking?

This kind of strategy is particularly useful in terms of reinforcing the need to gather accurate evidence. Explain to the group that what we believe about ourselves is not always true. It is not how others always see us and these kinds of beliefs need to be challenged in this way. Using this sort of questioning process, and gathering evidence in the form of such a behavioural experiment, is a particularly positive strategy for beginning to identify and challenge unhelpful beliefs that young people may carry.

6.2 Time to reframe

Discuss in the group how it is possible for negative thoughts can be reframed into more **positive**, **balanced** and **realistic** ones.

For example:

'I am just fat', could be reframed as:

I need to lose some weight and tone up a bit, but my overall shape isn't that bad.

'I always get the maths work wrong', could be reframed as:

Some of these sums are difficult, but I know I can do the basics – I just need to work hard and find help in order to improve my skills.

Worksheet 6.3, 'Time to Reframe', asks people to choose three negative thoughts and reframe them into new and more positive thoughts. If anyone gets stuck, they could work with a partner as sometimes it can be very helpful for a trusted friend to challenge a negative thought from their outside perspective.

Remind the group that the process of reframing their negative thought is about coming up with a **positive**, **balanced** and **realistic** thought.

Reflections Worksheet

This is a personal activity to be completed individually, since it asks young people to identify the negative thought they have most often and then to test whether or not it is true. Part of the worksheet can be completed in the session and the follow-up in the next session or at home once they have tested their negative thought.

Give each person Reflections Worksheet 6, 'Test Your Thought!', and ask them to think of the negative thought that they have most often, and then to rank it on a scale of 0 to 10 for how true they think it is (where 0 is least likely to be true and 10 is most likely to be true). Next they must come up with a way of testing how true their thought is and carrying this out (e.g., 'I am ugly and fat and everyone hates me', could be tested by recording for one week all the times people said good or kind things to me and did not make nasty comments about my weight or appearance). Ask them to consider what they think might happen if their thought is true.

Once they have conducted their experiment, they can record what actually happened and then rescore their thought according to how true they now believe it to be and compare this score with the original.

Discussion & Feedback

Ask the group to reflect on what they have learnt during the session, and in particular on the following questions:

- What have you learned about negative automatic thoughts or NATs?
- Is it easier to challenge our own negative automatic thoughts or those of others? Why is this?
- How can we 'test the evidence' in our everyday lives?
- How can we create more positive habits?

Worksheet 6.1
Using Cognitive Behavioural Therapy (CBT) Skills

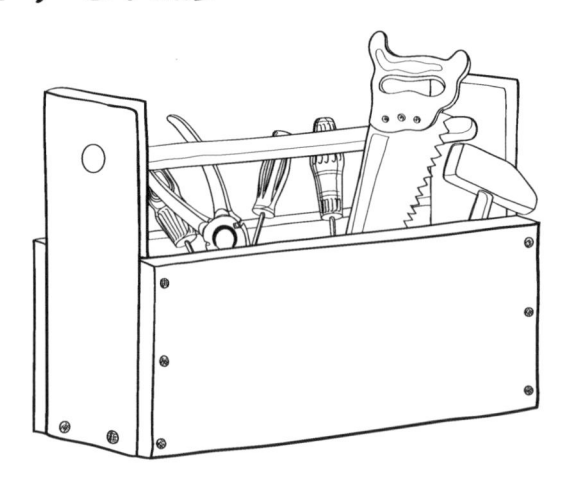

Your personal toolbox to cope with stresses and find the best solutions

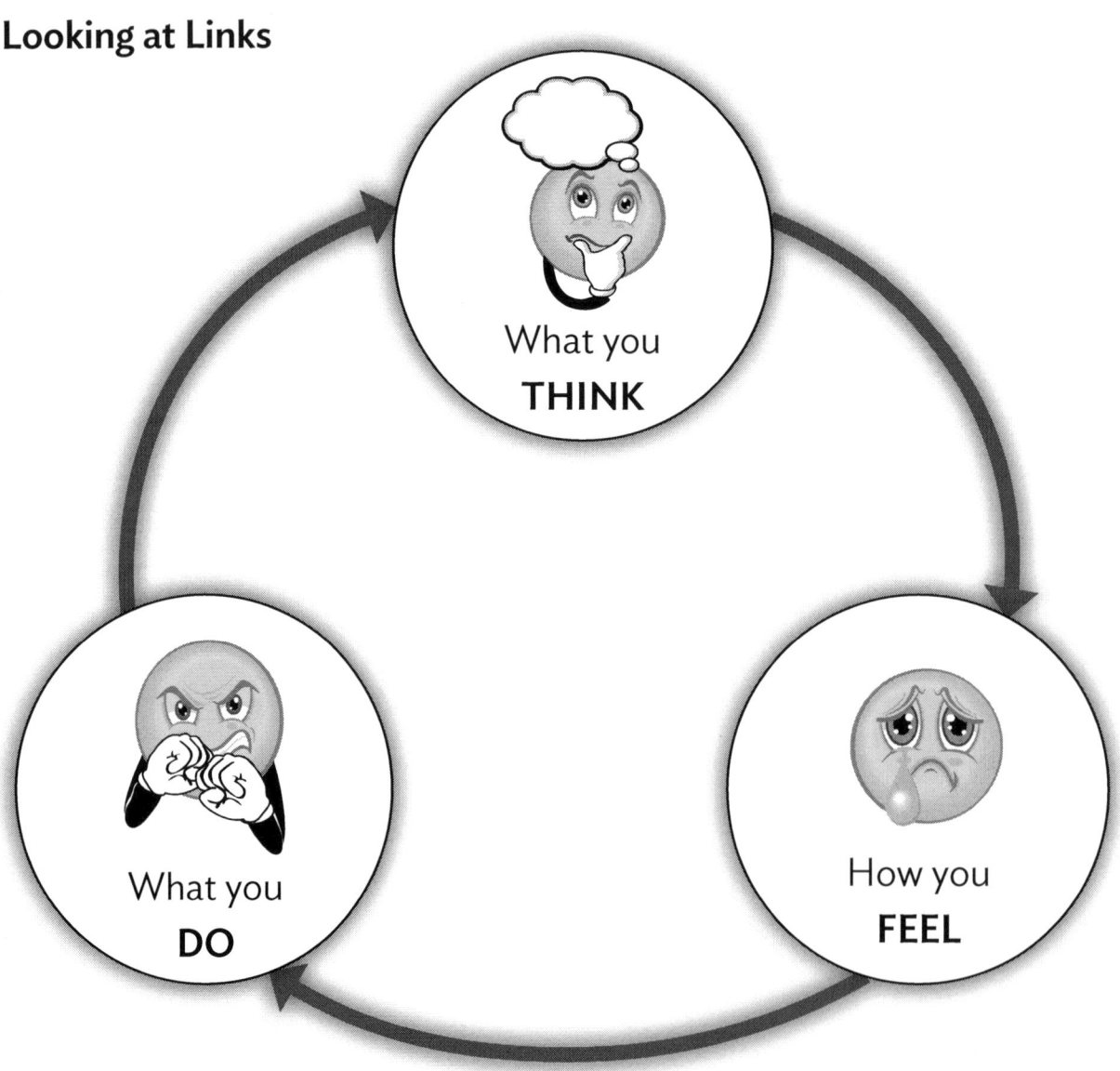

Looking at Links

- What you **THINK**
- How you **FEEL**
- What you **DO**

Cognitive Behavioural Therapy (CBT)

How links work

Some examples:

Think ... ⟶	Feel ... ⟶	Do ...
I'm useless at meeting new people.	I feel scared and nervous when I meet new people.	I don't talk to them and go quiet.
No one wants to talk to me.	I feel hurt and sad.	I avoid people at break times and start to skip school.
I'm rubbish at English.	I feel stupid and frustrated.	I won't do the work because I know I'll get it wrong anyway.

FACT! How you think about something will become true.

Stop – Think – Reflect

Time to ask ...

- Is this true?
- Can we change the way we think?
- Can we handle our problems differently to change how we feel and what we do?
- Can we gain more CONTROL over what happens to us in our lives?

Worksheet 6.2
Testing the Evidence

In the box below write a negative thought that you have about yourself:

```
┌─────────────────────────────────────────┐
│                                         │
│                                         │
│                                         │
└─────────────────────────────────────────┘
```

Then ask yourself:

1 What is the evidence for this thought?
   ➤ _____
   ➤ _____
   ➤ _____

2 What is the evidence against this thought?
   ➤ _____
   ➤ _____
   ➤ _____

3 What would my best friend say if they heard my thought?
   _____

4 What would my teacher say if they heard my thought?
   _____

5 What would my parents or carers say if they heard my thought?
   _____

6 What would I say to my best friend if they had this same thought?
   _____

7 Am I making mistakes in my thinking? For example, blowing it up, forgetting my strengths or good points, self-blaming or predicting failure, or thinking that I can mind-read what others are thinking?

   _____
   _____
   _____

Worksheet 6.3
Time to Reframe

Negative thoughts can be reframed into more **positive**, **balanced** and **realistic** ones.

Examples:

'I am just fat' could be reframed as:

I need to lose some weight and tone up a bit, but my overall shape isn't that bad.

'I always get the maths work wrong' could be reframed as:

Some of these sums are difficult, but I know I can do the basics – I just need to work hard and find help in order to improve my skills.

'I am rubbish at working with others because I am too shy' could be reframed as:

I sometimes get nervous in a group but I can be more comfortable if I take a deep breath and focus on the task and not on what I think people are thinking or saying about me.

Write three negative thoughts on the next page of the Worksheet, then shift them across and reframe them into new and more **positive** thoughts.

Worksheet 6.3 Time to Reframe

Negative thought →

Negative thought →

Negative thought →

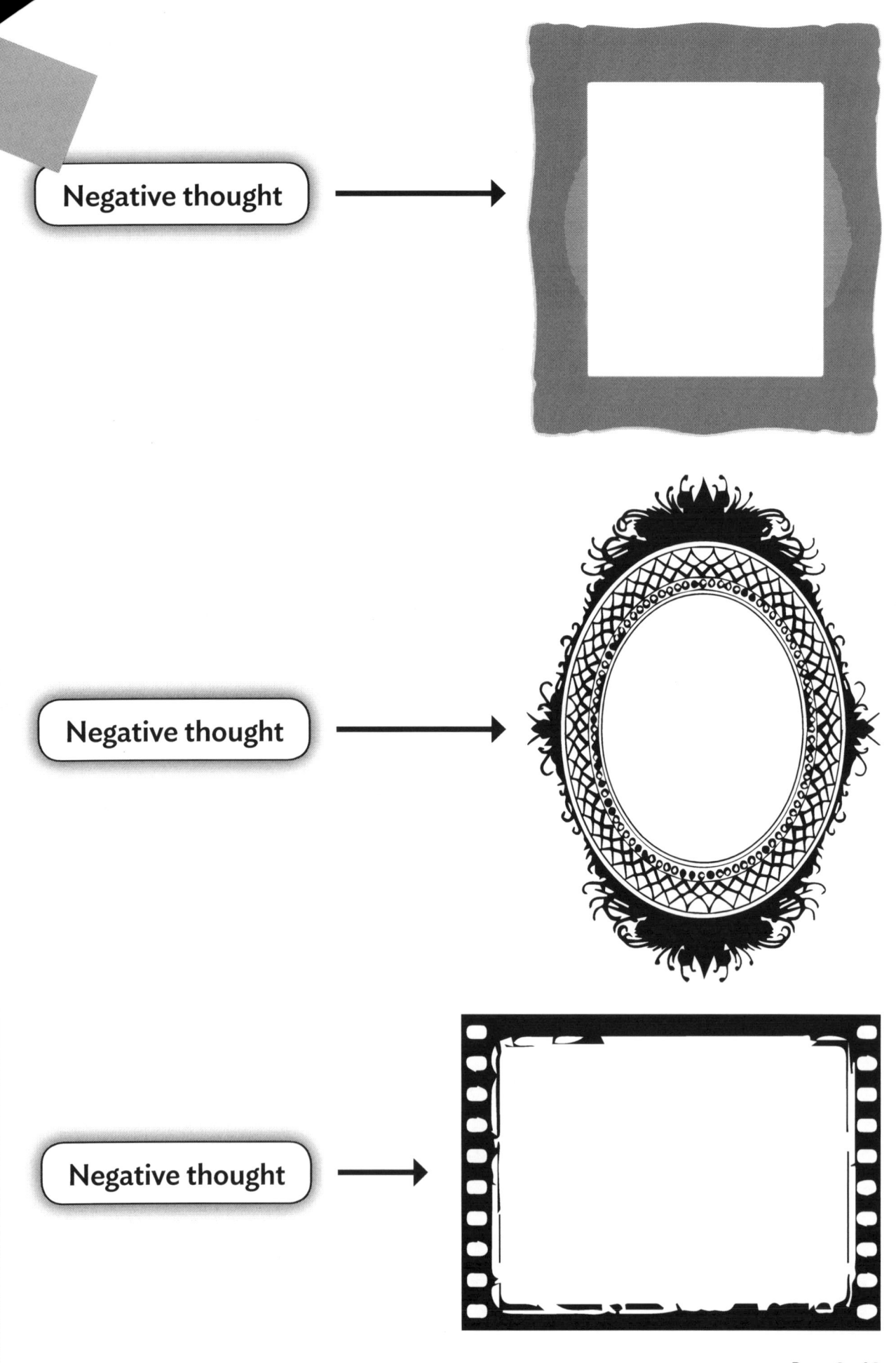

Page 2 of 2

Reflections Worksheet 6
Test Your Thought!

▶ Identify the negative thought you have *most* often:

[   ]

▶ **SCALE IT!**

Mark your thought out of 10 for how strongly you believe this thought
(0 = not strongly; 5 = quite strongly; 10 = extremely strongly)

0 1 2 3 4 5 6 7 8 9 10

▶ Design an **EXPERIMENT!**

What test could you set up to see if this is true?

_____
_____

▶ When will you do this?

_____

▶ If you think your negative thought is true, what do you think will happen?

_____
_____

AFTERWARDS...

▶ What *did* happen?

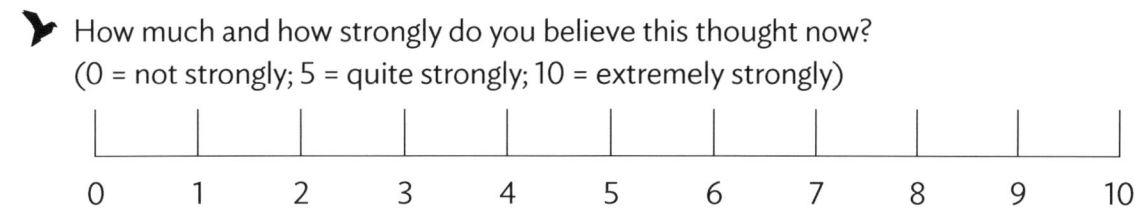

_____
_____

▶ How much and how strongly do you believe this thought now?
(0 = not strongly; 5 = quite strongly; 10 = extremely strongly)

0 1 2 3 4 5 6 7 8 9 10

Session 7

Using Tools from Positive Psychology to Create a More Positive Mindset

Introduction

In this session the group will be introduced to the ideas emanating from positive psychology.

Positive psychology preoccupies itself with the components of subjective well-being. This is the technical term for what we would call 'happiness' and the factors that enable us to grow, develop and sustain ourselves in a positive manner. A key factor is the focus on what actually works for us as individuals, as opposed to the continual analysing of what has gone wrong, or what we are not good at. The goal of positive psychology is to enhance human strengths, such as optimism, courage, honesty, self-understanding and interpersonal skills. This is the opposite of what has been called 'focusing on the broken things and on repairing the damage of past traumas' (Seligman, 2006).

Positive psychology provides a means of helping people to use their inner resources as a buffer against setbacks and adversity in life whenever these crop up. Developing these skills helps to prevent individuals from becoming depressed. As Seligman says, 'It's not about how to heal; it's about how to have a great life'. Using positive psychology can enable schools to become inspiring, comforting, fun and exciting. When schools make use of these strategies to build optimistic environments where positive emotions are promoted and young people's emotional resilience is fostered, then academic, social and emotional gains will be made by all involved.

Central to any positive psychology approach in schools is that young people should have optimum opportunities to experience positive emotions. This will ensure their ability to attend to lessons, increase working memory and verbal fluency and also ensure an increased openness to information (Seligman, 2006). Seligman highlights three essential areas that are key to happiness and well-being, which should also improve learning in the classroom. These are:

1 Hope & optimism

Young people will learn if they feel hopeful about their own skills and their future. Optimism ensures that both young people and adults can develop resiliency skills – the ability to bounce back from adversity and remain in control of their own emotions and behaviours. Resiliency is something that develops through positive relationships and it is vital that the young people have at least one adult who believes totally in their worth and abilities. This adult should also have the capacity and commitment to redirect the young person towards being productive, successful and happy.

2 Flow

Flow is defined as a sense of deep engagement in an activity, during which time passes extremely quickly and the individual is able to work at full capacity. Nothing distracts them as they learn and make progress towards their ultimate goals. The aftermath to this state is truly invigorating as the individual will feel happy and relaxed with a sense of achievement. This is something that we should strive for with all our students. However, translating this kind of absorption into more formal learning settings can be a challenge, in that it is easier to achieve flow in activities that are self-selected and intrinsically enjoyable. What is essential is that the challenge is relevant to the task. If it is too great, the student will feel anxious or frustrated, whereas when it is appropriate (in other words, there is a good balance between level and skill), then the young person will succeed and begin to achieve this state of flow.

3 Happy memories

Happy memories are extremely important and, as Seligman states, '… the way that we feel about the past and our experiences can clearly impact both positively and negatively on how we feel and function at the present time'. Students in classrooms who only remember how badly they did last time are likely to underperform in the present. Ideally, teachers need to encourage students to pay attention to what they did well and what they got right, particularly when struggling with new challenges. It is extremely important to ensure that young people are able to build and use happy memories, whilst also reframing negative automatic thoughts. Young people need to be taught to (a) monitor these negative narratives and be mindful of whether or not their thoughts are helpful or discouraging, and (b) nurture the positive stories they tell themselves on a regular (i.e., daily) basis.

Icebreaker

Give each person a copy of Worksheet 7.1, 'Feeling Good & Flourishing'. Discuss the points on the worksheet in the group and then ask everyone to focus on what they can all do in order to a) Feel good and b) Flourish. Record the group's responses on a flipchart or whiteboard and discuss these in the whole group.

Activities

7.1 Character strengths

Discuss in the group how we all have different character strengths, which can be broadly grouped under different headings, and how these are important to all aspects of our lives, not just within school. Give each person Worksheet 7.2, 'Character Strengths Information Sheet', to read and discuss in pairs or small groups. Ask each group member to pick one character strength from each section that they feel is particularly important to them and to share why this is so.

7.2 My 24 character strengths

Explain to the group that they are going to focus on their own character strengths and rate them on a scale of 1 to 10, where 0 is a very weak characteristic and 10 is a very strong characteristic.

Ask everyone to look carefully again at Worksheet 7.2, 'Character Strengths Information Sheet', to ensure they understand the meanings of the different strengths. Now they should each think about their own strengths. Using Worksheet 7.3, 'My 24 Character Strengths', they should rate each one on the scale and then try to identify their top two character strengths.

7.3 My top two character strengths: an analysis

Using Worksheet 7.4, 'My Top Two Character Strengths: An Analysis', each person should record their two top character strengths in the boxes and write about how these strengths show up in their lives and the times that they use them.

7.4 Building resilience: Using strengths to cope with problems

Discuss in the group that we can use our character strengths to help us to find solutions to problems and so stop ourselves from becoming stressed and anxious.

Worksheet 7.5, 'Building Resilience: Using Strengths to Cope with Problems', asks the group to think of a recent problem that they have solved and then to think about which three of their character strengths they used to find the solution or overcome the problem.

Discuss responses in the whole group; is anyone surprised to find that they have strengths they were not aware of before? How might these strengths be used again in the future?

Reflections Worksheet

Ten keys to happier living

There are 10 'keys' to happier living given on Reflections Worksheet 7, 'My Ten Keys to Happier Living'. The first five focus on how we interact with the outside world and the second five come from within us. Look at these 10 keys very carefully. Think about what you understand each of these 'keys' to mean for you in your life. Try to record the things that you do against each of the headings and make a plan to build on these every day of the week.

Giving	Do things for others
Relating	Connect with people
Exercising	Take care of your body
Appreciating	Notice the world around
Trying out	Keep learning new things
Direction	Have goals to look forward to
Resilience	Find ways to bounce back
Emotion	Take a positive approach
Acceptance	Be comfortable with who you are
Meaning	Be part of something bigger

Discussion & Feedback

Ask group members to write down three positives they have learned about themselves during this session. You can invite young people to share these if they would like to, but since this is a quite personal exercise, they may want to keep their thoughts private.

Worksheet 7.1
Feeling Good & Flourishing

The Greek philosopher Aristotle thought that people need to feel good and to flourish in order to achieve true happiness.

Feeling good and **Flourishing**

Feeling good is about having positive feelings, experiencing pleasure and good relationships.

Flourishing is the result of living a good and meaningful life. You flourish when you feel that you are leading a good life and when others think you are too.

Things we can do to feel good	Things we can do to flourish
Have fun!	Develop our talents!
Challenge negative thoughts!	Be future focused!
Keep fit!	Set good goals!
Have positive relationships!	Make a positive contribution to others!

Worksheet 7.2
Character Strengths Information Sheet

Wisdom & Knowledge: strengths that are all about learning and using new knowledge

1. **Creativity:** Thinking of new and interesting ways to do things.

2. **Curiosity:** Taking an interest in what is going on in the world and wanting to find out about new things.

3. **Judgement:** Thinking things through carefully before making up your mind, weighing up all the evidence carefully, and being able to change your mind when you get new information.

4. **Love of learning:** Learning new skills and information and enjoying finding out more about the things that you already know.

5. **Perspective:** Being wise and looking at the world in a way that makes sense and being able to give others good advice.

Courage: emotional strengths and being able to overcome difficulties and reach one's goal

6. **Bravery:** speaking up for what is right, not running away when things get difficult.

7. **Perseverance:** finishing what you start, keeping going even if things are difficult, and enjoying finishing tasks.

8. **Authenticity:** speaking the truth and being genuine and true to yourself.

9. **Taking responsibility:** owning your feelings and actions and not blaming somebody else when things go wrong.

Love: interpersonal strengths, looking out for and being a friend to others

10. **Intimacy:** enjoying being close to people.

11. **Kindness:** helping others and taking care of them.

12. **Social intelligence:** understanding what makes other people tick; knowing how to fit in and behave in lots of different situations.

Page 1 of 2

Justice: dealing fairly with people

13 **Teamwork:** working well as a member of a team; being loyal to the group and doing your share.

14 **Fairness:** treating all people fairly and giving everybody a fair chance.

15 **Leadership:** Encouraging your team or group to get things done; organising activities and making sure that they happen.

Temperance: not overdoing things

16 **Forgiveness:** forgiving those who have done wrong and giving people a second chance.

17 **Modesty:** not 'bigging' yourself up, not seeking the spotlight, not thinking that you are more special than you are.

18 **Prudence:** making careful choices, not taking big risks, not saying or doing things that you will later regret.

19 **Self-control:** controlling your behaviour, not being too emotional, not eating too much.

Transcendence: strengths that make connections to the universe and provide meaning in life

20 **Awe:** noticing and appreciating beauty and things done well, for example, the skills and talents of yourself and others.

21 **Gratitude:** being aware of and thankful for the good things that happen to you; taking time to say thank you.

22 **Hope:** expecting the best in the future and working towards it; believing that a good future is something that can be built.

23 **Playfulness:** liking to laugh and play; bringing smiles to other people, sharing a joke and a laugh.

24 **Spirituality:** having beliefs about the meaning of the universe and about life that shape one's behaviour and provide comfort.

Worksheet 7.3
My 24 Character Strengths

Look carefully at the Character Strengths Information Sheet.

Think about YOUR strengths. Rate each one on the scale and identify your TOP character strengths.

1. I am creative and think of new ways to do things.

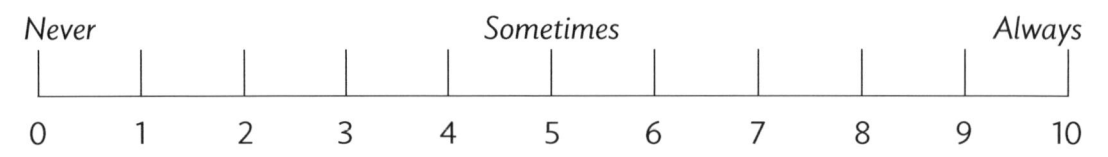

   Never   Sometimes   Always

   0   1   2   3   4   5   6   7   8   9   10

2. I am curious and want to find out new things.

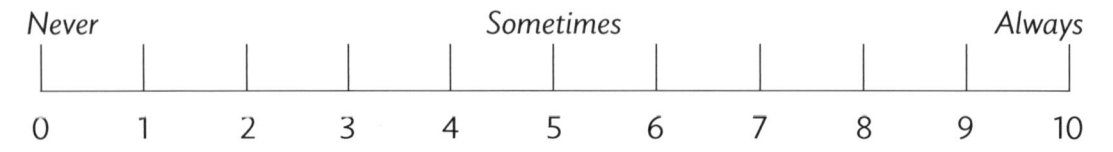

   Never   Sometimes   Always

   0   1   2   3   4   5   6   7   8   9   10

3. I use my judgement and think carefully before making decisions.

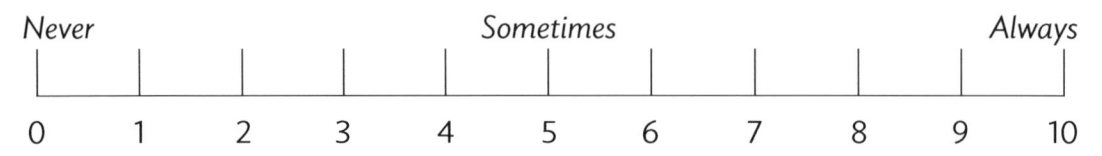

   Never   Sometimes   Always

   0   1   2   3   4   5   6   7   8   9   10

4. I love learning and finding out new things.

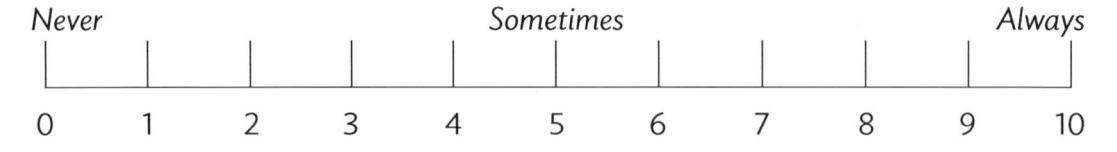

   Never   Sometimes   Always

   0   1   2   3   4   5   6   7   8   9   10

5. I keep things in perspective and don't make problems worse.

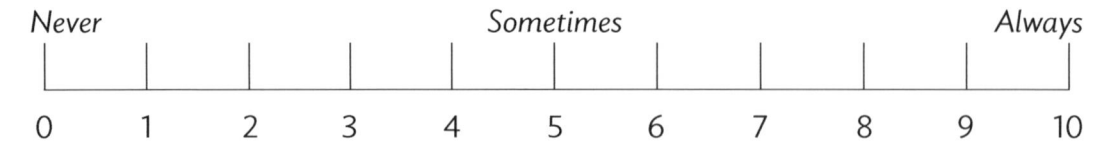

   Never   Sometimes   Always

   0   1   2   3   4   5   6   7   8   9   10

6. I am brave and will face up to problems.

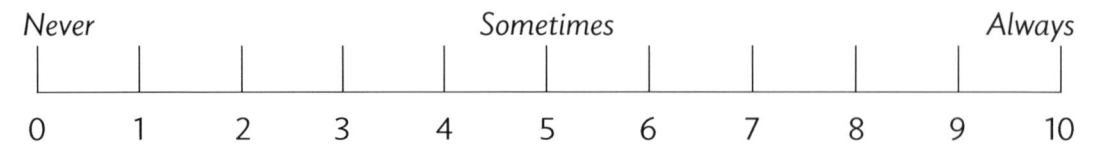

   Never   Sometimes   Always

   0   1   2   3   4   5   6   7   8   9   10

7 I finish off things I start, even if things get hard.

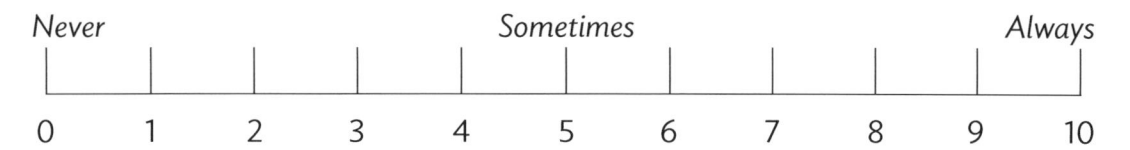

Never Sometimes Always
0 1 2 3 4 5 6 7 8 9 10

8 I tell the truth – to myself and to others.

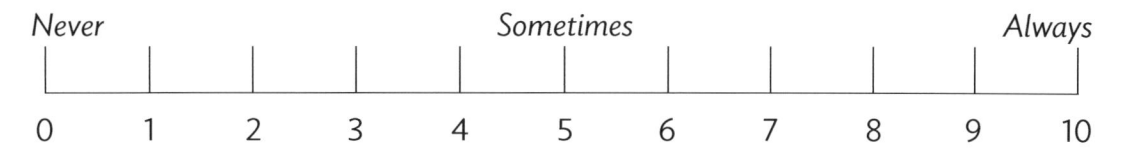

Never Sometimes Always
0 1 2 3 4 5 6 7 8 9 10

9 I am responsible for my actions and don't blame others.

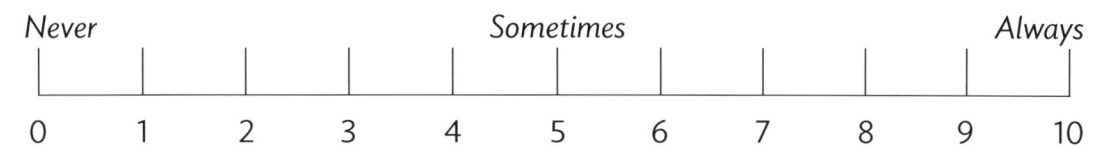

Never Sometimes Always
0 1 2 3 4 5 6 7 8 9 10

10 I like being close to other people.

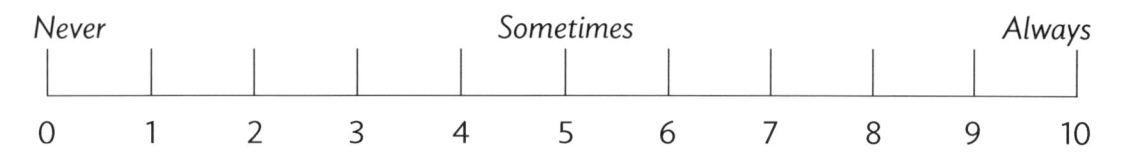

Never Sometimes Always
0 1 2 3 4 5 6 7 8 9 10

11 I am kind to others and take care of them.

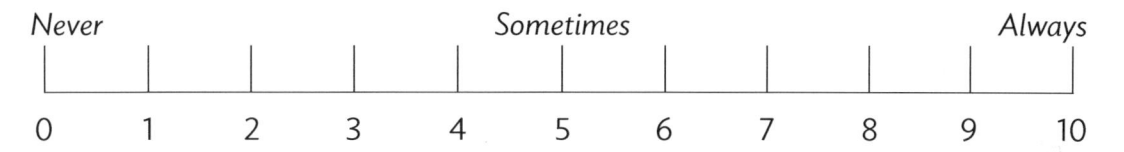

Never Sometimes Always
0 1 2 3 4 5 6 7 8 9 10

12 I understand what makes other people behave as they do and can 'fit in' with them when I need to.

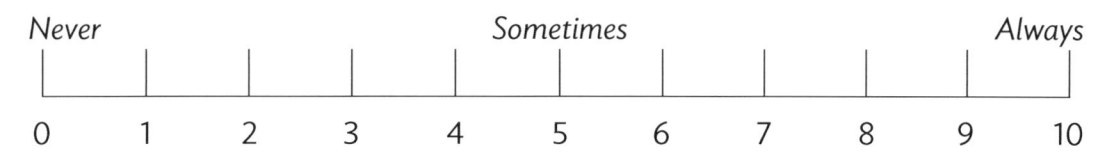

Never Sometimes Always
0 1 2 3 4 5 6 7 8 9 10

13 I work well in a team and am loyal to the group.

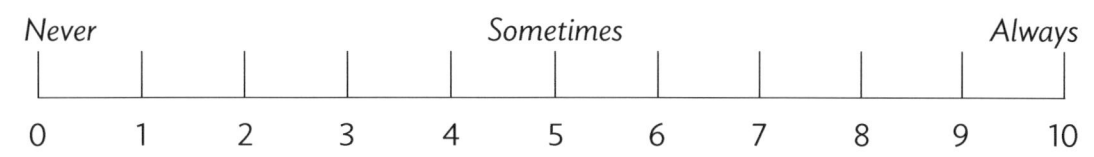

Never Sometimes Always
0 1 2 3 4 5 6 7 8 9 10

Worksheet 7.3   My 24 Character Strengths

14 I treat people fairly.

Never · · · · Sometimes · · · · Always
0   1   2   3   4   5   6   7   8   9   10

15 I am good at being a leader.

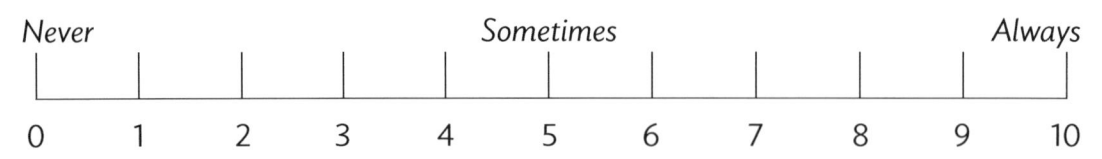

Never · · · · Sometimes · · · · Always
0   1   2   3   4   5   6   7   8   9   10

16 I forgive people and give them a second chance.

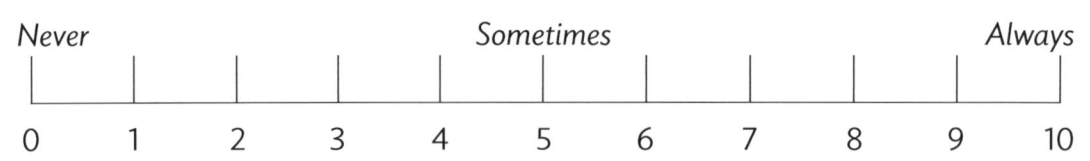

Never · · · · Sometimes · · · · Always
0   1   2   3   4   5   6   7   8   9   10

17 I am modest about myself and my achievements.

Never · · · · Sometimes · · · · Always
0   1   2   3   4   5   6   7   8   9   10

18 I make careful choices and don't take big risks.

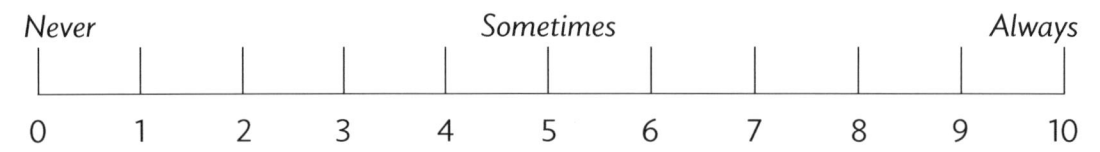

Never · · · · Sometimes · · · · Always
0   1   2   3   4   5   6   7   8   9   10

19 I control my feelings and behaviours.

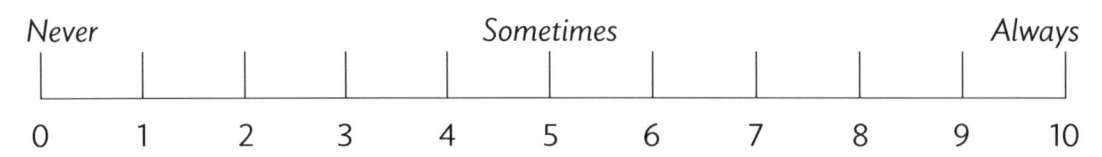

Never · · · · Sometimes · · · · Always
0   1   2   3   4   5   6   7   8   9   10

20 I know when things are beautiful and well done.

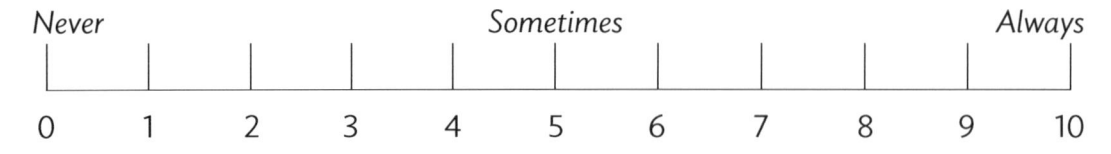

Never · · · · Sometimes · · · · Always
0   1   2   3   4   5   6   7   8   9   10

21 I am thankful for the good things that happen to me and say thank you.

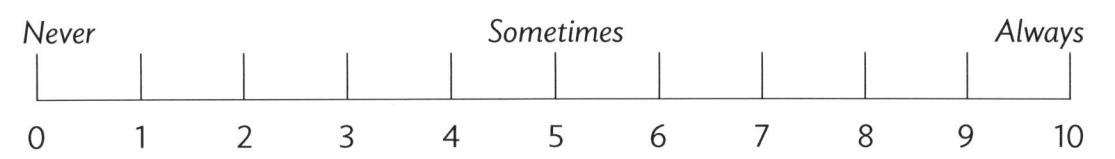

Never   *Sometimes*   *Always*

0   1   2   3   4   5   6   7   8   9   10

22 I expect a good future and know I can make it happen.

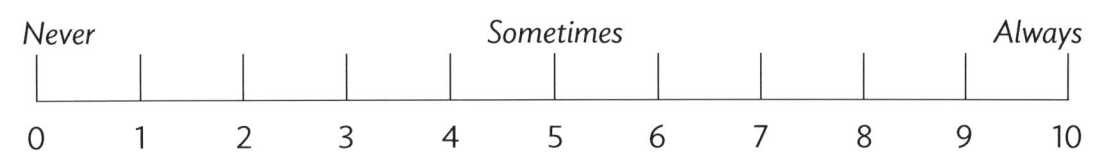

Never   *Sometimes*   *Always*

0   1   2   3   4   5   6   7   8   9   10

23 I enjoy laughing and making others smile.

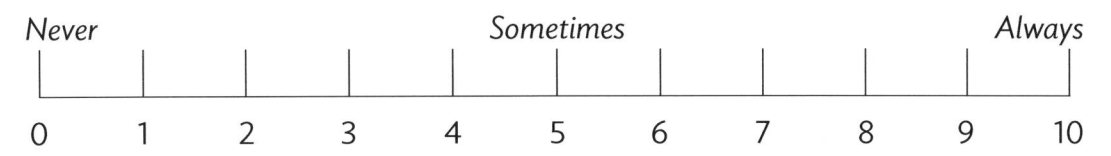

Never   *Sometimes*   *Always*

0   1   2   3   4   5   6   7   8   9   10

24 I have a set of beliefs which help me to understand myself and the world.

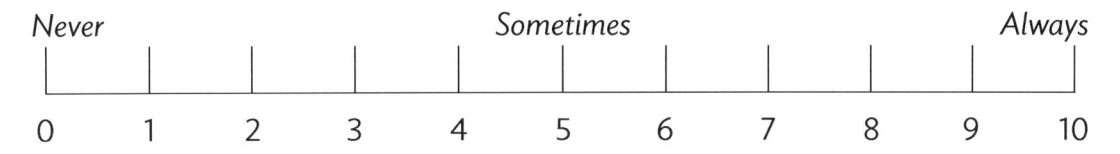

Never   *Sometimes*   *Always*

0   1   2   3   4   5   6   7   8   9   10

(Adapted from Seligman & Peterson, 2004)

Worksheet 7.4
My Top Two Character Strengths: An Analysis

Record your two top character strengths in the boxes and write about how the two strengths show up in your life, and the times that you use them.

My top strength is _____
_____

I am aware of it in my life when _____
_____

When I am using this strength I feel this is the 'real' me.   Yes   No

Time goes very quickly when I am using this strength.   Yes   No

I feel excited when I am using this strength, because things go well for me.   Yes   No

It is easy for me to use this strength.   Yes   No

New ways of using this strength are:

1 _____
_____

2 _____
_____

3 _____
_____

Page 1 of 2

My next top strength is _____

I am aware of it in my life when _____

When I am using this strength I feel this is the 'real' me.	Yes	No
Time goes very quickly when I am using this strength.	Yes	No
I feel excited when I am using this strength, because things go well for me.	Yes	No
It is easy for me to use this strength.	Yes	No

New ways of using this strength are:

1 _____

2 _____

3 _____

Worksheet 7.5
Building Resilience: Using Strengths to Cope with Problems

You can use your character strengths to help you to solve problems and find solutions.

Describe a problem situation you have dealt with recently.

List three character strengths that enabled you to sort this situation out:

1 _____

2 _____

3 _____

Explain how you used each of your strengths:

1 I used my first strength to _____

2 I used my second strength to _____

3 I used my third strength to _____

What happened?

Reflections Worksheet 7
My Ten Keys to Happier Living

Listed below are 10 keys to happier living.

The first five focus on how we interact with the OUTSIDE world and the second five come from WITHIN us.

Look at these 10 keys very carefully. Think about what you understand each of these keys to mean for you in your life.

Now think about the last week – what have you been up to? Try to come up with two or three examples for each key that you have done in the last week and write them in the box.

Key	Meaning	My Examples
Giving	Doing things for others.	
Relating	Connecting with people.	
Exercising	Taking care of your body.	
Appreciating	Noticing the world around you.	

Page 1 of 2

Reflections Worksheet 7 — My Ten Keys to Happier Living

Key	Meaning	My Examples
Trying out	Keeping learning new things.	
Direction	Having goals to look forward to.	
Resilience	Finding ways to bounce back.	
Emotion	Taking a positive approach.	
Acceptance	Being comfortable with who you are.	
Meaning	Being part of something bigger.	

Now go back to each one and, in a different coloured pen or pencil, come up with a new example of something you could do in the coming week.

Session 8

Breaking the Cycle & Moving Forwards

Introduction

It is possible for everyone to learn to live without needing to self-harm, but for some it can be a lengthy and difficult journey. The longer someone self-harms, the harder it can be to break the pattern of behaviour, but with the right support, understanding and motivation it is possible for everyone to find a good place of recovery. An important step forward is making the decision to learn to live without self-harm, and being prepared to face underlying issues that may have caused the behaviours in the first place. No one can make someone 'get better'. Hiding sharp objects, medicines or anything else thought to be harmful will not stop someone from self-harming unless they want to stop.

In this final session the group are introduced to the importance of establishing new and more positive habits and stepping away from negative but familiar ways of coping. This process requires self-awareness and for the group to reflect on many of the themes they have engaged with in previous sessions. This session is focused on the future and next steps, and how the young people will take forward the positive strategies they already use and the new ones they have identified.

Icebreaker

Give each person a copy of Worksheet 8.1, 'Self-Acceptance Checklist', and ask them to work through the list and give each statement a rating from 1 to 10, where 1 is 'not at all' and 10 is 'totally'. Ensure that you emphasise that there are no right or wrong answers. The focus of this session is on knowing yourself, because this is really important in helping us to make positive steps forward.

Before starting the checklist, discuss the characteristics of people who accept themselves and have good self-esteem. These people:

- Have certain values they believe in, act on and can defend. At the same time they are secure enough to alter these, if they need to.
- Are able to act in their own best interests without excessive guilt. If they make 'mistakes' they are able to accept this and learn.
- Value themselves and see themselves as being of value to others, particularly to those with whom they associate.
- Are sensitive to the needs and feelings of others.
- View others positively, looking for the best in them.
- Remain confident in their ability to deal with problems, even when things seem to be going badly.
- Feel equal to others as a person – not superior or inferior – irrespective of the differences in abilities, backgrounds or attitudes.
- Accept praise without false modesty or rejection.
- Resist the efforts of others to dominate them or put them down.
- Accept the range of desires and feelings they experience – positive and negative. It does not follow from this that they will act on all desires and feelings.
- Do not worry unduly about the future or past.

Once everyone has completed their checklist, they can discuss their answers with a partner, thinking about what they can do to develop or improve their levels of self-acceptance and self-esteem.

Activities

8.1 When people don't feel like harming themselves

Give each group member a copy of Worksheet 8.2, 'When People Don't Feel Like Harming Themselves'. Ask them to read through the questions and think about how their answers might be helpful in supporting someone to break the cycle of self-harm.

8.2 Prevention or safety plan review

In Session 4 members of the group created their own personal prevention or safety plans and this activity allows them the opportunity to review those plans in light of their own experiences and the subsequent sessions. Ask everyone to look through their safety plans from Session 4 and to ask themselves:

- What has changed for me?
- What has stayed the same?
- What have I tried?
- What works for me?
- How would I like to change my safety plan?

Then give each person a copy of Worksheet 8.3, 'My Personal Self-Harm Prevention or Safety Plan', so that they can draw up their plans again, having considered their experience during the sessions.

Reflections Worksheet

Reflections Worksheet 8, 'Course Evaluation & Feedback', should provide useful information for both you and the school and can inform the content and delivery of future courses.

Ideally both parts of the worksheet should be completed individually, but you could also take course feedback from the group once the personal feedback sheets are completed, if time allows.

Worksheet 8.1
Self-Acceptance Checklist

Rate yourself against each statement on a scale of 1–10
(1=not at all; 5=a medium amount; 10=totally)

People who accept themselves and have good self-esteem:

- Have certain values they believe in, act on and can defend. At the same time they are secure enough to alter these, if they need to.

   0   5   10

- Are able to act in their own best interests without excessive guilt. If they make 'mistakes', they are able to accept this and learn.

   0   5   10

- Value themselves and see themselves as being of value to others, particularly to those with whom they associate.

   0   5   10

- Are sensitive to the needs and feelings of others.

   0   5   10

- View others positively, looking for the best in them.

   0   5   10

- Remain confident in their ability to deal with problems, even when things seem to be going badly.

   0   5   10

Worksheet 8.1 Self-Acceptance Checklist

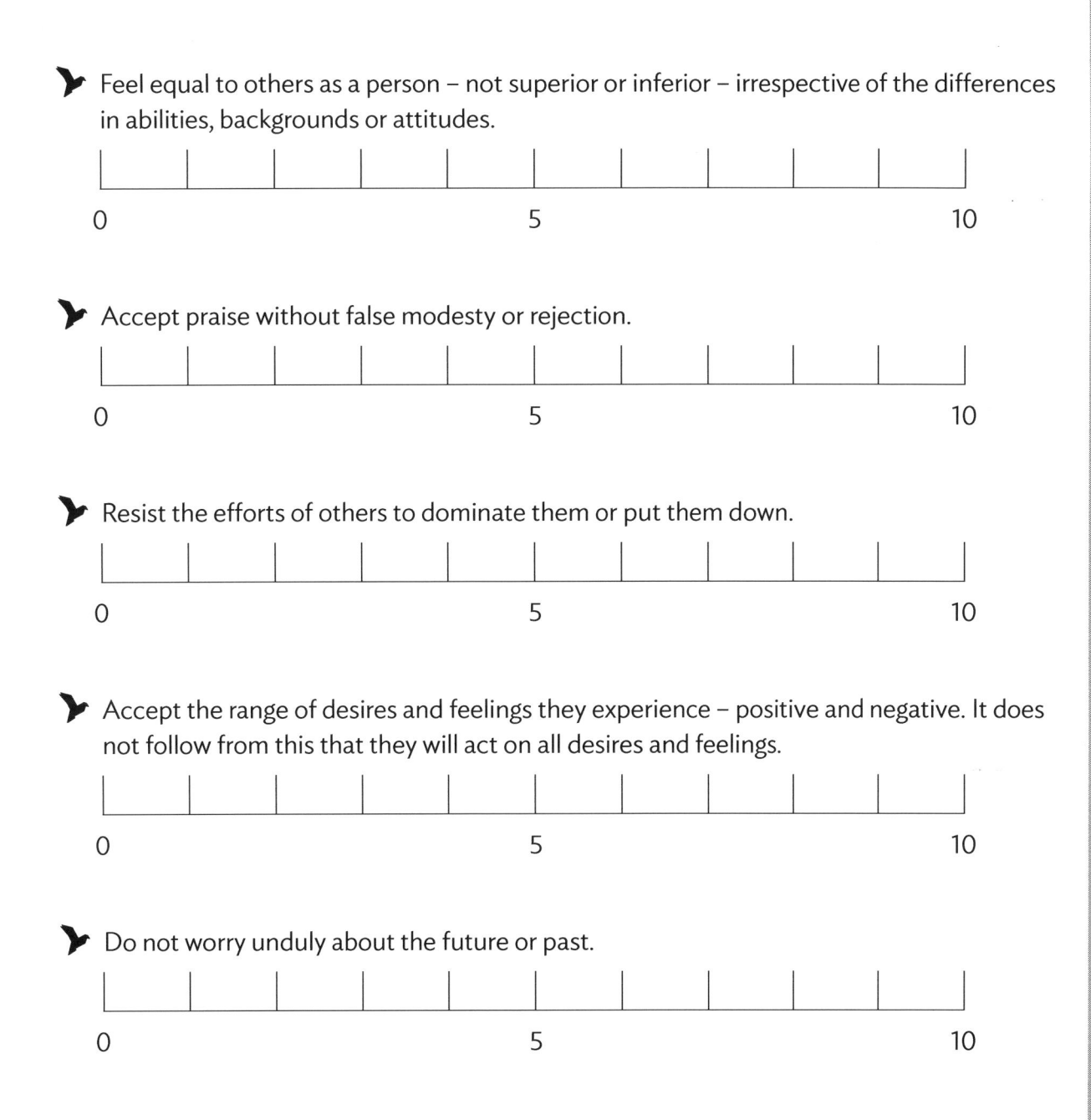

➤ Feel equal to others as a person – not superior or inferior – irrespective of the differences in abilities, backgrounds or attitudes.

|__|__|__|__|__|__|__|__|__|__|__|
0   5   10

➤ Accept praise without false modesty or rejection.

|__|__|__|__|__|__|__|__|__|__|__|
0   5   10

➤ Resist the efforts of others to dominate them or put them down.

|__|__|__|__|__|__|__|__|__|__|__|
0   5   10

➤ Accept the range of desires and feelings they experience – positive and negative. It does not follow from this that they will act on all desires and feelings.

|__|__|__|__|__|__|__|__|__|__|__|
0   5   10

➤ Do not worry unduly about the future or past.

|__|__|__|__|__|__|__|__|__|__|__|
0   5   10

How do you need to develop or improve your levels of self-acceptance and self-esteem? Discuss your thoughts with a partner.

Worksheet 8.2
When People Don't Feel Like Harming Themselves

The following list contains some strategies that people might use to stop themselves from self-harming the next time they feel stressed or anxious. Read these through and think about which might be helpful in supporting a friend who self-harms.

> When you are in a peaceful state and feel safe, go back in your mind to the last time when you wanted to self-harm; then move forward in your memory from there.

> Think about where you were, who you were with, and what you were feeling that last time.

> Try to work out why you began feeling like you did.

> Did your self-harm give you a sense of escape, or relief, or control? Try to work out something to do that might give you the same result, but that doesn't damage you.

> How did other people react?

> Could you have done anything else?

> Make an audio recording. Talk about your good points and why you don't want to self-harm. Or, ask someone you trust to do this. When you start to feel bad, you can play this back to remind yourself of the parts of you that are good and worthwhile.

> Make a 'crisis plan' so you can talk to someone instead of self-harming. Being able to get in touch with someone quickly can help you control your urge to self-harm. While you are talking, your wish to harm yourself may start to go away.

Worksheet 8.3
My Personal Self-Harm Prevention or Safety Plan

What makes me want to harm myself? For example, it could be particular people, feelings, places or memories.

[ ]

Other than harming myself, what else helps me to cope?

[ ]

What would I tell a close friend to do who was feeling this way?

[ ]

Worksheet 8.3 My Personal Self-Harm Prevention or Safety Plan

What could others do that would help?

[   ]

If I feel like harming myself again, I will do one of the following
(try to list 6-8 items):

1. _____
2. _____
3. _____
4. _____
5. _____
6. _____
7. _____
8. _____

If the plan does not work and I still feel like harming myself, I will do at least one of the following:

- Call the *Samaritans* on **116 123** (free calls)
- Call *ChildLine* on **0800 1111** (free calls)
- Talk to a trusted adult _____
- Call emergency services **999** or go to nearest A&E

Signed: _____   Date: _____

Reflections Worksheet 8
Course Evaluation & Feedback

This feedback will not be shared with the group, but will provide useful information for your group leader or teacher to help them plan future courses.

Rate the following statements on a scale of 1–10
(1 is 'I strongly disagree', and 10 is 'I totally agree').

I understand what is meant by 'self-harm'.

1	2	3	4	5	6	7	8	9	10
disagree				neither agree or disagree					agree

I can identify my own self-harming behaviours.

1	2	3	4	5	6	7	8	9	10
disagree				neither agree or disagree					agree

I can identify stressors in my life.

1	2	3	4	5	6	7	8	9	10
disagree				neither agree or disagree					agree

I have skills for coping with stress in my life and a crisis plan for when things get tough.

1	2	3	4	5	6	7	8	9	10
disagree				neither agree or disagree					agree

I could support a friend who is self-harming.

1	2	3	4	5	6	7	8	9	10
disagree				neither agree or disagree					agree

I can identify triggering images and content on social media or websites.

1	2	3	4	5	6	7	8	9	10
disagree				neither agree or disagree					agree

I can name helpful and unhelpful responses to stress and anxiety.

1	2	3	4	5	6	7	8	9	10
disagree				neither agree or disagree					agree

My Evaluation of the Sessions

Finish the following sentences.

The activity I enjoyed most was _____
_____
_____

The activity I enjoyed least was _____
_____
_____

Something I have learned is _____
_____
_____

I would like to learn more about _____
_____
_____

The most useful part of the sessions was _____
_____
_____

The least useful part of the sessions was _____
_____
_____

Something I would change about the sessions is _____
_____
_____

Any other comments _____
_____
_____
_____

Part 3

Resources

A Developing a Self-Harm Policy

B Sample School Self-Harm Policy

C Information Leaflet for Parents, Carers & Young People

D Sample Letter to Parents & Carers Explaining the Course

E Sample Letter to Young People Explaining the Course

F Sources of Help, Support & Information

G Information to Include in a CAMHS Referral

H Initial Conversations Around Self-Harm or Suicidal Thoughts with a Young Person

Resource A

Developing a Self-Harm Policy: Notes to Support Staff

Why Have a School Policy on Working with Students who Self-Harm?

Often self-harm is not taken seriously enough. We want to believe it is a passing phase, attention seeking, or simply that it is not happening in our schools. But with as many as one in ten teenagers self-harming (which could be as many as three in every tutor group), there is clearly a strong need to have a standardised and consistent approach to supporting those who self-harm in our schools. This is necessary in order to give all school-based staff confidence about how to respond to cases of self-harm and all service users the confidence that incidents of self-harm are dealt with through a clearly thought-out system of support. By creating a self-harm policy a school will also audit its current systems for dealing with self-harm and highlight training needs within the organisation.

The Purpose of the Policy

The policy should set out clear guidelines on procedures for dealing with those who self-harm, both in the short and long term. These need to be in keeping with the school's overall values, vision and aims. However, a comprehensive policy will also consider how issues such as raising self-esteem and developing emotional literacy will be addressed throughout the school. It should provide information on support systems for staff who are dealing with those who self-harm, when outside agencies should be contacted, and how to prevent self-harm from spreading within the school. The education of both students and staff should be addressed, as well as guidelines for involving parents with regard to individual cases.

Preparing the Content of the Policy

The actual content of a school's policy must be individual to reflect each institution's ethos and procedures. However, consideration of the following points may be useful:

1 What is our understanding of self-harm?

It is essential that definitions of self-harm are included in the policy and distinctions should be made between self-harm with and without suicidal intent, in order to have a shared understanding and philosophy amongst all staff. Indicators and risk factors should be clearly outlined and information on all of this is included in the Introduction to this book.

2 Responding to individuals who self-harm: roles and responsibilities

The head teacher and the governing body

The head teacher has a responsibility to appoint a designated member of staff for dealing with incidents of self-harm (this is often the child protection officer).

The head teacher and governing body should ensure that a policy is in place, and that it is communicated to all staff and implemented across the school. In order for any policy to be effective it is important to have input from key stakeholders. These include staff at all levels and particularly pastoral leaders. This will help ensure the resulting policy is acceptable, suitable and feasible.

Consideration should be given to the training needs of all staff regarding self-harm, especially those of the designated staff member, and how these are to be met. Information will need to available to staff regarding self-harm and sources of advice and help. The head teacher will need to determine what information will be available and how this will be accessed.

All staff and teachers

If an individual discloses that they self-harm, how do you want staff to respond? For example, they should listen in a non-judgemental way.

- Sources of help and support should be provided for the student, as well as information and facts about self-harm.
- The designated staff member should be informed. The policy should state the timescale within which this is expected to happen.
- Staff should not make promises which they may not be able to keep. For example, 'we can sort it out'. This obviously may not be possible. Similarly, staff should not promise confidentiality, but should reassure the student that they will be kept informed at all times of any action that is to be taken.
- If an incident of self-harming has occurred on the premises, medical attention may be necessary. All staff should be aware of the procedures for accessing first aid help within the school.

- If the behaviour of the student is deemed to be suicidal, an emergency response will be necessary. What are such emergency procedures?
- What support will be provided for staff and to whom will they go if they need guidance in a particular situation?

The designated staff member

The designated staff member will have responsibility for recording all incidents of self-injury and will determine the most appropriate course of action, which might include contacting parents and arranging professional assistance.

- Consideration will also need to be given as to what information, if any, will need to be shared amongst other staff members and how this is to be done.
- The designated member of staff will have a duty to keep up to date with information regarding self-injury and forms of support and services available. They should inform parents about any appropriate help and support that is available for their child.
- The student should be involved in the process of dealing with the disclosure or incidence of self-harm and the designated staff member should closely monitor the student throughout and following this process.

Preventing the Spread of Self-Harm within a School

In some instances where there has been a case of self-harm, the behaviour can be triggered in others. To prevent such a spread the following may be useful:

- Wounds, injuries and scars should not be openly displayed.
- Provision of uniform items such as long-sleeved PE kits may be necessary for those who do self-harm.
- The designated member of staff should try to identify 'high status' peers who may be self-harming, and mapping out a sociogram may be helpful in this respect.
- Where deliberate coercion is found to be present, such as providing a pen-knife for another to try self-harming, disciplinary action may be necessary.

Implementing and Reviewing the Policy

The communication of the policy is key to its successful implementation. All staff will need to be aware of its existence and content, but it is equally important that parents and students are made aware of the policy. Parents need to work in partnership with the school when supporting students who self-harm and endorse its approach to the education of students regarding self-harm. Students need to be confident that if they disclose information regarding self-harm, either by themselves or a friend, that it will be dealt with competently and sensitively.

The policy should be reviewed regularly in line with all related policies, which may include: the behaviour policy, child protection policy, health and safety policy and SEN policy.

Resource B
Sample School Self-Harm Policy

This Policy is divided into 5 sections:

1. Purpose of the Policy
2. Definitions of Self-Harm
3. Aims of the School Team with Regard to Self-Harm
4. Key Responsibilities
5. Links to Other Policies

1 Purpose of the Policy

In keeping with the School's vision and aims, this Policy aims to address the issue of self-harm; it covers the following areas:

- How to deal with pupils who self-harm and how to offer support in the short and long term;
- How to provide support depending upon the individual needs of the pupil;
- How to help all pupils improve their self-esteem and emotional literacy;
- How to support staff members who come into contact with people who self-harm;
- How to prevent self-harm from escalating within the school;
- Providing clear guidelines for staff on who needs to be informed and when parents and outside agencies need to be contacted;
- Providing education about self-harm for pupils and staff.

2 Definitions of Self-Harm

Self-harm is considered to be a coping mechanism for young people who are attempting to deal with high levels of distress and emotional pain. It may be defined as any deliberate, non-suicidal behaviour that causes physical pain or injury and is aimed at reducing the emotional pain and distress of the individual concerned.

These behaviours may include deliberate bone-breaking, cutting, bruising, banging and non-suicidal overdosing, and the behaviours are usually chronic, repetitive and habitual. Young people who self-injure will generally attempt to hide any scarring or injuries and can find it extremely difficult to discuss their behaviours, and the emotions behind them, with others. We understand these behaviours not to be about seeking attention, but rather to be about seeking relief and release from emotional distress.

We also understand that self-injury is not suicidal behaviour. However, the emotional distress that causes these behaviours can lead to suicidal thinking and actions – we will consequently take ALL incidents of self-injury seriously, investigate them, and attempt to provide the most appropriate emotional support possible.

Suicide

While self-injury and suicide are separate, those who self-injure are in emotional distress and those who choose to end their lives are also in emotional distress. It is vital that all emotional distress is taken seriously to minimise the chance of self-injury and suicide. All talk of suicide and warning signs must be taken extremely seriously.

Actions following discovery of a suicide risk

1. Following a report of a risk of suicide from a pupil, the SMT in discussion with the pastoral care lead will decide on the appropriate course of action. This is likely to include:
   - Contacting parents or carers;
   - Arranging professional assistance;
   - Immediately removing the student from school if their presence in class is likely to cause further distress to themselves or their peers. Alternatively, seeking reassurance that it is in their best interests and in the interests of the wider community that they remain in school and that it is safe for them to do so.

2. The pupil will remain in the care of their parents or carers until the school receives sufficient evidence that the pupil is not a significant risk to themselves or others under the normal levels of supervision in a day school. The head teacher may direct and require parents to make use of relevant professional and medical services.

3. The school will usually require additional safeguards following a pupil's return, which may include a commitment to attend appointments with counsellors, the GP, and/or CAMHS.

3 Aims of the School Team with Regard to Self-Harm

Our school team is dedicated to ensuring the emotional, physical and mental well-being of all pupils who attend. We consequently aim to:

1. Recognise any warning signs that one of our pupils may be engaging in self-harming behaviours;
2. Understand the risk factors associated with these behaviours, including low self-esteem, perfectionism, mental health issues such as anxiety or depression, home or school problems, social isolation, emotional, physical or sexual abuse;
3. Be pro-active in discussing this topic with pupils we might feel are deliberately harming themselves;
4. Know how to respond to pupils who wish to discuss these behaviours with us and take them seriously at all times;
5. Be able to produce short- and long-term care and management plans for such pupils, in conjunction with external agencies if necessary;
6. Provide the appropriate level of practical and emotional support for staff dealing with pupils who self-harm and ensure appropriate training and education is available to all staff regarding this issue.

Recognising warning signs

We are aware that for some young people there will not be any specific warning signs that they are engaging in or contemplating engaging in self-harming behaviours. For others, the following indicators may be noted:

1. Risky behaviours, for example, drug taking, alcohol misuse;
2. Lack of self-esteem, being overly negative;
3. Bullying of others;
4. Social withdrawal;
5. Significant change in friendships;
6. Regularly bandaged wrists and arms;
7. Obvious cuts, burns or scratches (that don't look like accidents);
8. A reluctance to participate in PE or change clothes;
9. Frequent accidents that cause physical injuries
10. Wearing long-sleeved tops even in very hot weather.

4 Key Responsibilities

- Everyone in the school community – the school governors, the head teacher, SMT, all staff and teachers, pupils and parents – has a responsibility to promote and adhere to this policy in order to help ensure the well-being of all within the community. These responsibilities are outlined below.
- Any member of staff who is aware of a student engaging in, or suspected to be at risk of engaging in, self-harm should consult the health centre staff and the senior deputy head.
- **In the case of an acutely distressed student, the immediate safety of the student is paramount and an adult should remain with the student at all times.**
- **If a student has self-harmed in school the health centre or 999 should be called for immediate help.**

Governors undertake to do the following:

1. Ensure the existence of a Procedural Policy in case of self-harming incidents occurring within the school context and that this is reviewed as necessary;
2. Bear ultimate responsibility for the school's role in maintaining pupil health and well-being;
3. Have nominated governors in charge of safeguarding;
4. Ensure that safeguarding and child protection issues are regularly reported to the governors;
5. Put in place appropriate safeguards on admissions to maintain a tolerable level of risk with regard to the health and well-being of pupils.

The head teacher undertakes to do the following:

1. Keep the governors aware of major incidents and trends;
2. Appoint a designated member of staff to be responsible for all incidents of self-harm and be responsible for disseminating the policy and training;
3. Be ultimately responsible for ensuring that designated staff members receive appropriate training, support and supervision;
4. Ensure that all staff in the school community are fully conversant with and adhere to this Self-Harm Policy.

Designated staff will do the following:

1. Ensure that the Policy is disseminated and implemented appropriately, providing regular feedback and updates to the head teacher;
2. Develop a record-keeping system to record such incidents and ensure that this is kept up to date and incidents and developments are regularly reported to the head teacher;
3. Ensure that pupils have an appropriate care and management plan which is recorded and, if necessary, developed with the support of external specialist agencies;
4. Liaise with external agencies (specifically mental health) in order to provide the most appropriate support, alongside utilising key services to provide up-to-date education and information for pupils, parents or carers and staff;
5. Liaise with parents or carers as appropriate in order to ensure the safety and well-being of pupils in the school community;
6. Report on suicidal intent or feelings straight away and refer to other professional bodies as appropriate;
7. Engage in appropriate supervision so as to ensure personal well-being.

All staff undertake to do the following:

1. Act in an empathetic manner, assuring pupils that they are available to listen in a calm and non-judgmental manner;
2. Not invalidate any pupil's concerns or emotional distress;
3. Know the available support options or referral routes and refer pupils to these as appropriate;
4. Ensure that pupils know that staff cannot make any promises to keep things confidential if they feel that the pupil is at risk. **If staff consider a student is at serious risk of harming themselves, then confidentiality cannot be kept. It is important not to make promises of confidentiality that cannot be kept even if a student puts pressure on a staff member to do so;**
5. Adhere to all other relevant and associated school policies;
6. Be committed to providing an emotionally literate context in which the self-esteem and emotional and mental well-being of all are fostered and promoted;
7. Be aware of the 'healthy' coping strategies pupils can utilise and know who to ask for advice if it is felt that these are being abused or becoming unsuccessful for the pupil;
8. Ask for help if they feel a situation falls outside of their emotional competency, skills or knowledge base;

9. Encourage students to pass on information if one of their group is in trouble, upset or showing signs of self-harming. Friends can worry about betraying confidences so they need to know that self-harm can be very dangerous and that by seeking help and advice for a friend they are taking responsible action and being a good friend. They should also be aware that their friend will be treated in a caring and supportive manner;

10. Be aware that the peer group of a young person who self-harms may value the opportunity to talk to a member of staff either individually or in a small group. Any member of staff wishing for further advice on this should consult the Designated Safeguarding Lead (DSL);

11. Be vigilant when a young person is self-harming, in case close contacts with the individual are also self-harming. Occasionally schools discover that a number of students in the same peer group are harming themselves.

Students may choose to confide in a member of school staff if they are concerned about their own welfare, or that of a peer. School staff may experience a range of feelings in response to self-harm in a student, such as anger, sadness, shock, disbelief, guilt, helplessness, disgust and rejection. However, in order to offer the best possible help to students it is important to try to maintain a supportive and open attitude – a student who has chosen to discuss concerns with a member of school staff is showing a considerable amount of courage and trust.

Staff should go to the DSL for support and help following incidents covered in this policy to help protect their own well-being.

Parents or carers need to do the following:

1. Ensure that they both understand and endorse this policy;
2. Find out about self-harm, making use of school-based and external resources, and discuss findings with the child;
3. Ensure that appropriate school staff members are kept informed of any changes or incidents that occur outside the school that may have an impact on the behaviour and well-being of the child;
4. If the child is engaging in these behaviours, work with designated staff in order to help the school develop the best ways of supporting the child and his or her parents or carers;
5. Recognise that they may also need emotional support and find out where this is best accessed.

Pupils must do the following:

1. If self-harming, they will take care of any wounds appropriately and not display them in the school context. Pupils failing to comply with this requirement once appropriate support is in place may face sanctions under the school's Behaviour Management Policy;

2. Ensure that they do not engage in 'sensationalised' conversations with peers or staff or talk about the methods they use to other pupils. Pupils failing to comply with this requirement once appropriate support is in place may face sanctions under the school's Behaviour Management Policy;

3. Try to find something fun and positive in each day;

4. Never encourage others to participate in self-harm;

5. Focus on the emotional issues and not on the act of self-harm itself.

6. Ensure that they know who they can talk to in both the immediate and longer term, should they feel distressed or at risk in either the school or social context;

7. Alert a member of staff if they are at all concerned about a friend or peer who may be at risk of self-harming, engaging in these behaviours, or who may present as suicidal or discussing suicide.

5 Links to Other Policies

Our Self-Harm Policy has direct links to (and should be read in conjunction with) the following related policies, all of which are available on the intranet:

- Health and Safety Policy
- Behaviour Management Policy
- Safeguarding and Child Protection Policy
- Special Educational Needs Policy
- Anti-Bullying Policy

This Policy will be monitored by [insert as appropriate] and reviewed after requesting evaluative feedback from all key stakeholders. This will enable us to make the relevant and appropriate changes and ensure that this policy remains useful and user friendly.

Resource C
Self-Harm: Information for Parents, Carers & Young People

This leaflet provides information about self-harm and is intended to be helpful to young people and their friends and families.

What is Self-Harm?

Self-harm is a major public health issue among young people in the UK.

It is something that affects at least 1 in 15 young people, making their lives extremely difficult and seriously affecting their relationships with friends and family.

Self-harm describes a range of things that people do to themselves in a deliberate and usually hidden way. It might involve:

- Taking too many tablets
- Cutting
- Burning
- Banging or scratching one's own body
- Breaking bones
- Hair pulling
- Swallowing toxic substances or inappropriate objects

These things are not done in a calculated way, as some people might erroneously think. Someone who self-harms does this in a state of real distress and unbearable emotional pain. Some people may self-harm only on a few occasions, while for others it will become a regular thing – like an addiction.

Who Self-Harms and Why?

The average age for young people to begin self-harming is 12 years old and the majority of people who self-harm are aged between 11 and 25 years. It is more common in young women than men, and those who self-harm are more likely to have experienced an emotional trauma or possibly physical, emotional or sexual abuse during childhood. Factors leading to self-harming may include:

- Feeling isolated and/or depressed
- Relationship problems with partners, friends and family
- Academic pressures
- Low self-esteem and feeling hopeless
- Physical or sexual abuse
- Being bullied
- Feeling powerless (as though there's nothing you can do to change anything)
- Using alcohol or drugs
- Needing to show someone else how distressed you are in order to punish them (this is not the norm though – most people are very private about the whole process)

Can Self-Harm Among Young People Be Prevented?

There is now an increasing amount of evidence to show that there are ways of preventing self-harm among young people. There are lots of initiatives in schools, for example, anti-bullying strategies and whole-school approaches to promote the emotional health and mental well-being of young people, which seem to help. However, there is no evidence as yet that these initiatives have any real impact upon self-harming behaviours.

Evidence from young people themselves would suggest that social isolation is a key factor for some. They also tend to think they are the only person who self-harms. However, when accessing so called self-harm sites, they can begin to see themselves as part of a self-harm community and this has its own dangers, in that it normalises their behaviours to some extent and can therefore impede seeking help.

Better information and understanding can help to reduce or prevent these behaviours. This increased awareness needs to be shared by parents or carers and teachers and others who come into contact with young people. This is one of the main objectives of this leaflet; to equip young people, their parents or carers, and teachers with the information and support systems they need in order to more fully understand, cope with and ultimately reduce these self-harming behaviours.

What Help is There?

Young people themselves have suggested that finding ways to distract from self-harming behaviours really helps. Distraction techniques that are reported to be effective include: using a red pen to mark, rather than cutting; rubbing with ice; and hitting a punch bag.

There are also a wide range of services across the UK for young people who self-harm. These include:

- Problem Solving Therapy
- Cognitive Psychotherapy
- Psychodynamic Psychotherapy
- Cognitive Behavioural Therapy

Telephone help is given by:

- *Childline* – free national helpline for young people, free confidential advice on a range of problems (0800 1111)
- *NHS Direct* – a helpline with health advice provided by NHS Nurses (0845 4647)
- The *Samaritans* – A telephone helpline and email service for anyone who is feeling upset, worried, or suicidal (116 123, email jo@samaritans.org)

Resource D

Sample Letter to Parents & Carers Explaining the Course

Dear Parents or Carers,

As you may be aware the rates of self-harm and suicide amongst young people have risen in recent years. The safety and well-being of our students is a priority of our school and therefore we will address this issue in an eight-session programme this term.

The programme aims to raise awareness of the risk factors that may lead to self-harming behaviours. It will provide a safe framework in which students can develop their own preventative strategies and techniques for handling stress. The sessions will also focus on how students can support each other and access available support.

We hope you appreciate the importance of this programme for the personal, social and educational development of your child and that you will support them as they work through the programme.

Thank you.

If you have any concerns about this programme or require any further information please contact:

_____

Resource E
Sample Letter to Young People Explaining the Course

Dear _____

During this term we will be looking at the subject of self-harm in a course of eight sessions. We hope this leaflet answers some of the questions you may have about these sessions. If you have any further questions please discuss them with your form tutor or head of year.

What will We be Learning?

We will look at how events and stress in our lives may lead to self-harm. We will also develop our own strategies for handling stress and learn how to support our friends through difficult times.

What will I Gain by Taking Part in these Sessions?

You may find that concerns you have are similar to those of others in your class. You will learn strategies for handling stress and will have the opportunity to identify behaviours you may wish to change.

What will be Expected of Me?

You will be expected to be respectful of others in the class and keep any discussions confidential. You will be encouraged to listen and respond during group discussions, but you will not have to share any personal information.

We hope you enjoy the sessions and take the opportunity to try out new behaviours and attitudes.

Resource F
Sources of Help, Support & Information

British Red Cross Society: 0344 871 11 11

www.redcross.org.uk

Free training in camouflaging scars.

Changing Faces Skin Camouflage Service: 0300 0120275

www.changingfaces.org.uk/Skin-Camouflage

For someone living with scarring or a skin condition that affects their appearance and confidence, specialist camouflage products offer a way to cope. Our service helps individuals to regain self-confidence and independence. Runs around 120 clinics across the country.

Childline: 0800 1111

www.childline.org.uk

A free help, support and advice service for all young people.

Dabs Directory & Book Services: 01255 852774

24-hour answerphone helpline: 07854 653118

www.dabs.uk.com

Wide range of books relating to self-harm, child abuse, self-esteem, depression, etc.

Mind: 0300 123 3393

Text: 86463
www.mind.org.uk

Information and support for anyone experiencing a mental health problem.

National Self Harm Network

www.nshn.co.uk

Survivor-led organisation, with an online discussion forum aims to bridge the gulf in understanding and to campaign for the rights of those who live with self-harm. Leaflets have been produced for those who self-injure and for healthcare professionals.

Self-Injury Support

www.selfinjurysupport.org.uk

A national organisation that supports girls and women affected by self-harm. Services include:

CASS Women's Self-Injury Helpline: 0808 800 8088

For women of any age affected by self-injury and their friends, families and carers.

TESS Text and Email Support Service: 0780 047 2908

For girls and young women up to the age of 24 affected by self-harm.

SupportLine Telephone Helpline: 01708 765200

www.supportline.org.uk

Confidential emotional support for children, young people and adults. Keeps details of agencies, support groups and counsellors throughout the UK.

ZEST (N.Ireland): 0287 126 6999

www.zestni.org

Telephone counselling and other support services for individuals who self-harm or attempt suicide.

Useful Websites

http://alumina.selfharm.co.uk

Online course started by selfharm.co.uk for young people between 14 and 18 years. It doesn't matter how long you have been self-harming or what it means to you. *Alumina* is an opportunity to think more about it and work out what your next step might be.

www.havoca.org

For survivors of abuse, also deal with self-harm. Click on 'Information', then 'Self-Harm'.

www.lifesigns.org.uk

Self-injury guidance and network support.

www.nice.org.uk

National Institute for Clinical Excellence – national guidelines relating to treatment of self-harm. Put 'Self-Harm' in search bar at top of page.

www.recoveryourlife.com

A Suffolk-based self-harm community site offering support, companionship, information, advice, forum, message board.

www.selfharm.org.uk

Key information resource for young people who self-harm, their families, friends, and professionals working with them.

www.selfinjurysupport.org.uk

Information and advice, with list of support groups across the UK.

www.helplines.org.uk

Website of the Telephone Helplines Association giving information on helplines across the UK.

Resource G
Information to Include in a CAMHS Referral

Each CAMHS team may operate slightly differently, however, the more detail you are able to include in a referral the more likely they will be to make the most helpful decision for the young person and their family.

Information to include:

- The young person's symptoms.
- The impact of these symptoms on the young person's life.
- What is the context (e.g., recent life events, current stressors)?
- How long has it been going on for?
- Any other underlying difficulties?
- Any risk issues?
- What has already been tried to help them and what was the outcome?
- Family composition and anyone else who lives with the young person.
- Family background.
- Has there has been any social care involvement and, if so, details of the social worker involved.
- The attitude of the young person and their family to the referral.
- The family's contact details.
- School's contact details.
- GP's details.

Resource H

Initial Conversations Around Self-Harm or Suicidal Thoughts with a Young Person

If a young person discloses self-harm or suicidal thoughts, the following information can guide your discussion and act as a prompt to ensure that you cover key information that will be relevant for the safeguarding lead.

- Limitations of confidentiality. Be honest with the student and tell them you will have to pass this disclosure on to the designated safeguarding lead, but you will let them know what's going to happen and how you will keep them informed.

- Be clear with the student about how much time you have available for this conversation and the structure the conversation might take. For example, 'I'm glad you came to talk to me about this. I have half an hour now and we can talk about what has been going on for you and agree some next steps we can all put in place to support you.'

- Encourage the young person to remain in the setting until you have discussed the incident with the safeguarding lead.

- Try to ensure that if the young person is around in the setting for the rest of the day, they have someone they can talk to if necessary.

It is important to write down what the student says; however, it may not be appropriate to do this in front of them, so be sensitive. When making notes try to include exactly what the student says, rather than paraphrasing.

Self-Harm: Topics to cover

You have come to me and told me that you have self harmed ...

or

We are concerned you may have harmed yourself ...

Are you willing to show me what you have done? [It may need medical attention.]

or

What have you done?

Tell me about it? [Different types of self-harm: cutting, hitting, burning]

How did this make you feel?

Have you done it before?

Do you plan to do it again?

Have you told anyone else: your parents or carers or friends?

What are you planning to do the rest of the day/over the weekend?

[This is to check out if they have any support at home, or if they are going to be alone.]

Now this is out in the open this is what we need to do to support you ...

Suicidal Thoughts: Topics to cover

We believe that you have had these thoughts ...

or

You have come to me and told me that you have had these thoughts ...

Have you tried to do anything to harm yourself?

Have you made any plans to end your life?

What are you planning to do for the rest of the day or weekend?

References & Bibliography

Andersen J., Beels C. & Powell D., 1994, *Health Skills for Life. Health Education and PSE Materials for Key Stage 3*, Thomas Nelson & Sons Ltd., Edinburgh.

Andersen J., Beels C. & Powell D., 1994, *Health Skills for Life. Health Education and PSE Materials for Key Stage 4*, Thomas Nelson & Sons Ltd., Edinburgh.

http://www.cellogroup.com/pdfs/talking_self_harm.pdf

CHILDWISE 2015. 'Monitor Report 2015', CHILDWISE, Norwich.

Coleman J., 2004, *Teenage Suicide and Self-harm – A Training Pack for Professionals*, Brighton Trust for the Study of Adolescence, Brighton.

Department for Education and Skills, 2001, *Promoting Children's Mental Health within Early Years and School Settings*, DfEE Publications, London.

Department of Health, 2001, *Making It Happen. A Guide to Delivering Mental Health Promotion*, DoH Publications, London.

Dwivedi N. K. & Harper B.H. (eds), 2004, *Promoting the Emotional Well-Being of Children and Adolescents and Preventing their Mental Ill Health – A Handbook*, Jessica Kingsley Publishers Ltd., London & Philadelphia.

Faupel A., Herrick E. & Sharp P., 2001, *Anger Management – A Practical Guide*, David Fulton Publishers Ltd., London.

http://www.theguardian.com/society/2014/mar/10/self-harm-sites-cyberbullying-suicide-web

Hawton, K., 2015, *The All Party Parliamentary Group (APPG) on Suicide and Self-Harm Prevention. Inquiry into local suicide plans in England*. House of Commons, London.

Hawton, K., Harris L., Hall S., Simkin S., Bete E. & Bond A. (2003) 'Deliberate Self-Harm in Oxford, 1990–2000: a time of change in patient characteristics', *Psychological Medicine*, 33(6), 987–995.

Lindenfield G., 1995, *Self-Esteem. Developing Self-Worth. Healing Emotional Wounds*, Thorsons, London.

Martin R. & Whitehead C., 1994, *Speaking Out*, Health Education Authority, The Cromwell Press, Trowbridge, Wilts.

McKay M. & Rogers P., 2000, *The Anger Control Workbook*, New Harbinger Publications, Oakland, CA.

Meltzer H. & Gatward, R., 2000, *Mental Health of Children and Adolescents in Great Britain*, report of a survey carried out by the Office for National Statistics, The Stationery Office, London.

Mentality 2000, *Evidence Base – What Evidence Base? A review of some of the issues for Primary Health Care teams*, SCMH Annual Mental Forum – Mental Health Promotion and Primary Care Workshop.

NSPCC, 2000, *Child Maltreatment in the United Kingdom. A Study of the Prevalence of Child Abuse and Neglect*, NSPCC report, London.

NSPCC, 2015, *'Always There When I Need You'. What children are contacting ChildLine about*, ChildLine Review, London.

Open University, 1997, *Confident Parents Confident Children. A Community Education Study Pack*, Open University Press, Milton Keynes.

Rae T., 2016, *Bouncing Back & Coping with Change: Building Emotional & Social Resilience in Young People Aged 9–14*, Hinton House Publishers Ltd, Buckingham.

Rae T., 2016, *Building Positive Thinking Habits: Increasing Self-Confidence & Resilience in Young People through CBT*, Hinton House Publishers Ltd, Buckingham.

Rae T. & Bunn H., 2017, *The Essential Guide to Using Positive Psychology Approaches with Children & Young People*, Hinton House Publishers Ltd, Buckingham.

Rae T. & Giles P., 2017, *The Essential Guide to Using CBT Approaches with Children & Young People*, Hinton House Publishers Ltd, Buckingham.

Rae T., Walshe J. & Wood J., 2017, *The Essential Guide to Using Mindfulness Approaches with Children & Young People*, Hinton House Publishers Ltd, Buckingham.

Seligman M.E.P., 2006, *Learned Optimism: How to Change Your Mind and Your Life*, Vintage Books, New York.

Seligman M.E.P & Peterson C. (2004) *Character Strengths and Virtues: A handbook and classification*, OUP, Oxford.

Shaw C., 1998, *Remember My Messages – The Experiences and Views of 2000 Children in Public Care in the UK*, The Who Cares? Trust, Andus Print, Brighton.

The Mental Health Foundation, 1999, *Bright Futures. Promoting Children and Young People's Mental Health*, London.

Ward B. & Houghton J., 1988, *Good Grief. Talking and Learning about Loss and Death*, White Crescent Press, Luton.

Weare K., 2000, *Promoting Mental, Emotional and Social Health. A Whole School Approach*, Routledge, London.

WHO, 1986, *Ottawa Charter for Health Promotion*, WHO, Geneva.